55664                         791.8'4

STEINER, SID w/J. POMERANTZ

THEY CALL ME SID ROCK

| DATE DUE | | | |
|---|---|---|---|
| | | | |
| | | | |
| | | | |
| | | | |
| | | | |
| | | | |
| | | | |
| | | | |
| | | | |
| | | | |
| | | | |
| | | | |
| | | | |

✓

# They Call Me
# Sid Rock
## Rodeo's Extreme Cowboy

# They Call Me Sid Rock

## Rodeo's Extreme Cowboy

Sid Steiner

and

James Pomerantz

TRIUMPH
BOOKS
CHICAGO

Library of Congress Cataloging-in-Publication Data

Steiner, Sid, 1974–
    They call me Sid Rock : rodeo's extreme cowboy / Sid Steiner and James Pomerantz.
    p. cm.
    Includes index.
    ISBN 1-57243-627-1
    1. Steiner, Sid, 1974– 2. Rodeo performers—United States—Biography. 3. Steer wrestling.  I. Pomerantz, James. II. Title.

GV1833.6.S84A3 2004
791.8'4'092—dc22
[B]

2004044022

This book is available in quantity at special discounts for your group or organization. For further information, contact:

Triumph Books
601 South LaSalle Street
Suite 500
Chicago, Illinois 60605
(312) 939-3330
Fax (312) 663-3557

Printed in U.S.A.
ISBN 1-57243-627-1
Design by Patricia Frey

# Contents

# Foreword

Image is an illusion. The dictionary describes image as a likeness or imitation of a person or thing. The dictionary also categorizes image as a mental picture. For as long as I can remember, when an athlete has walked outside the company lines, that athlete has been tabbed "the bad boy" of the sport. I played my entire career in the National Football League with one single objective: I was on the field to win. I practiced hard to win when the games counted. I didn't play football to receive orders on how to dress and how to act from men I barely knew. My job was solely based on my production on the field, and I never signed a contract with the word puppet in the text.

The notion of unconventional has too often been synonymous with malicious. Remember, image is an illusion.

Unconventional behavior is not the prelude to malicious conduct. Individuality and personality do not lead to the seven deadly sins. Seventeen years ago, Bob Verdi and I wrote about the same subject. Joe Willie Namath set the stage years ago for a brash young BYU quarterback and later on for a headstrong Texas bulldogger.

Sid Steiner has angered many of the old established stalwarts of professional rodeo. They did not like his hair. They frowned on his tattoos and pierced ears and eyebrow. Sid Steiner had the audacity to wear leather pants and a black silk shirt to the National Finals. The hierarchy in rodeo would have preferred a military, boot camp haircut, a $20 pair of jeans, and a $5 shirt from Wal-mart. The "bad boy" of rodeo was going to ruin the sport. Sid Steiner went on to win the 2002 World Championship in Steer Wrestling with one of the most exciting 10th-round closing runs in Finals history. Sid Steiner had managed to bring an entirely new generation of fans into the sport of rodeo. Major sports hate it when thousands of new fans get excited about their sport.

Pete Rozelle, the commissioner of the NFL, and Michael McCaskey, the owner and managing partner of the Chicago Bears in the mid-eighties, made a habit of publicly denouncing whatever I was doing at the time to ruffle their shorts. I challenge anyone to name a team that generated more interest and attention than the 1985

World Champion Chicago Bears. How bad do you think the league and the owners of the most-watched team in NFL history wanted to stop the show? The almost forgotten aspect of the 1985 Bears team was not that we were an intimidating defensive unit, but that we controlled the ball for nearly 35 minutes per game. I had career highs for touchdowns and completion yardage. I concluded the season with a much-appreciated trip to the Pro Bowl in Honolulu. Excellence didn't simply fall from the sky. No one owed the Chicago Bears a title. We decided to pay the price necessary to cash in on a 22-year void. Bobby Steiner, Sid's father, won a Bull Riding World Championship in 1973. Sid Steiner decided to pay the price necessary to close a 22-year gap for the Steiner family.

I'll never claim to be an expert on rodeo. I can't say that I've ridden any bulls lately or thrown any steers. These days, I prefer a golf cart to any other means of transportation. Admiration extends across years and across any fields of endeavor. Sid caught my eye through a mutual friend, and I saw bits of myself in the tightly wound Texas cowboy. Behind the long hair and the wild tattoos is a man raised with tradition and Western values. Most of the established guidelines surrounding professional sports are worthless boundaries created by those too fragile to participate. Many athletes choose to walk within those guidelines. I respect their decisions and admire their quiet resolve. Others choose to walk the edge and wager the balance between performance and show. A select few hit the proverbial jackpot and walk away with a championship. I know the Sid Steiner mentality a little bit better than most!

—Jim McMahon

# Acknowledgments

## Buddies for Life

I've been lucky to have the opportunity to grow up and travel with some great guys. You're only as good as the company you keep. My childhood was made great with great friends. To all my little league baseball and football buddies that are still here for me today: Jeff Pool, Brian Walton, and Troy Smith. My high school buds: Justin Helms, John Scarborough, Brian Murray, Christian Foster, and Chris Cokins. Thanks for letting me always be myself and not judging me. I really think that "Sid Rock" was started at an early age.

Thanks Cuatro and Jason Hollen for always sticking with me through the good, the bad, and the ugly. (Cuatro knows about the last part.)

To Eddie Joseph for all those practices when everyone left but you. Thanks for the help, great times, and always making me laugh.

To Ethan Siegal for being a great friend and looking out for my bro.

To Jason Shelnutt for being the guy that everyone loves and always being there to have a beer with me.

To all my rodeo compadres.

To Todd Fox, thanks for the courage and advice.

To Brad LaRue, thanks for always keeping my spirits high and telling me I was great when I probably wasn't. You da man, Rudy.

To Butch Stokes, for seeing the talent in a hot-headed kid and helping me face my demons.

To Frank Davis, for being my friend from day one and letting me have the opportunity to rodeo with such a great person.

To Bryan Fields, for more things than I can mention, but most of all, for calming me down in times of need. Thanks, duuuuuuuuuude.

To Frank Thompson, for giving me the chance to be your friend when most probably wouldn't. You're a great friend and definitely a buddy for life.

To Alfalfa Fedderson, for all the great go's and great times, and for being the only cat farther out there than me. Love ya, Tex.

To Marvin Dubose and Alan Oehlert, for being great people and great friends and showing me the kind of person I can only hope to be.

To Byron Walker, for giving me wisdom.

To Luke Branquinho, for being the kid brother I never had and showing me your winning attitude.

A special note to Jim Pomerantz: sometimes in life there are just chance meetings. Some you remember, some you tend to forget. I guess you can say that the sport of rodeo has brought that about for me. How else would a brash guy like me from Texas hook up with an equally brash Yankee from Chicago? Thanks to you, Jim Pomerantz, for making me feel like the things that I have gone through are worth sharing. Our meeting is one I'll never forget. Hey Bam Bam, you rock!

# Introduction

During the first two weeks of December each year, the Las Vegas hotel marquees are saturated with country music legends and Nashville's newest mega-stars. The Western version of the World Series and the Super Bowl are rolled into a 10-day stretch called the Wrangler National Finals Rodeo. If you want a ticket to see any of the 10 rounds live at the Thomas and Mack Center, then you had to have put in your request 10 months ago. Otherwise, availability is limited to the numerous ticket brokers regularly squeezing out four to five times the face value of the tickets.

I have been to the National Finals Rodeo, or NFR, each year for the past decade. Late in 2000, I was completing my research at the NFR for a previous novel. The steer wrestlers had just completed their evening's competition.

One unique contestant had been raising the visibility of the event to unthinkable heights. Bull riding has generally been considered the most popular event within a rodeo. Steer wrestling, normally a tough sell and People for the Ethical Treatment of Animals' nemesis, has been the recipient of tremendous national media attention. Fan devotion akin to the four major sports and their chosen stars has been emerging at rodeo arenas throughout the country. Sid Steiner was fifth overall in the World Standings. At 26, rodeo's version of Brian Bosworth and Jim McMahon, "Sid Rock," was attracting young people to the sport like no one had since Lane Frost.

I wandered into the concession concourse at the Thomas and Mack Center to seek a tan-colored, frothy beverage. There was a commotion down the long hallway in front of me. Throngs of people were clumsily making their way toward me. As they approached, it was obvious that most of the individuals were women. They were clamoring after a young man with his black Stetson tipped back up on his head. The young man wore an NFR contestant's jacket. His hair hung down to his shoulders, and a small, silver ring hung precariously on his eyebrow. As the group reached a Professional Rodeo Cowboys Association (PRCA) sponsor's autograph table, I struggled to identify the source of the excitement. Then it became crystal clear. The cornrows struck me in Cheyenne. At Denver and San

Antonio, there were satin shirts and leather pants. A small sunburst tattoo adorned his chest and had been featured on the cover of *ProRodeo Sports News,* the sport's bible.

The young man sat at the sponsor table and took off his jacket. The autograph seekers hurried in some chaotic order to form a line that immediately stretched around the corner and out of view. The buzz filtered rapidly throughout the building. Females of all ages began to gavotte past the long-haired cowboy searching for the end of the line. The young cowboy wore a tight, short-sleeved shirt showcasing the ripped arms of a weightlifter. Fans were asking to have everything signed from hats, shirts, programs, and jackets to bras and panties. Tight jeans were tucked into custom-made alligator boots. One boot tapped along with the arena music as he signed every-thing placed on the table. One analogy that I imagined was Barry Bonds signing autographs between innings of a baseball game in progress. Another would be Bruce Springsteen signing autographs during a break in a concert. Giddy females clutched the newly ink-stained possessions and turned to catch one more glimpse of the brash smile. It was clear that the spotlight had finally found a mark in the exploding world of professional rodeo. Sid Steiner threw a 3.9 in the arena less than 20 minutes before his autograph session. The bad plaid shirts were gone. No one called Sid Steiner, "Tex."

Three years later, I have had the incomparable pleasure of working with Sid Steiner and his family for the better part of two years. A fourth generation Texan, Sid won the 2002 World Championship in Las Vegas on a breathtaking run during the final, or 10th, round. "Steer wrestling" or "bulldogging," is the sport of throwing steers. The event places the contestant on a quarter horse at full speed. The contestant will then slide off the horse at full speed to land on the horns of a 600-pound steer, also traveling at full speed. The contestant will then pile drive his heels into the arena floor while lifting and twisting the steer to the ground. The entire sequence of these events will unfold within four seconds if the contestant has any championship aspirations. A "hazer"—another cowboy who, riding a speedy quarterhorse, takes off from the opposite side of the steer—must ride simultaneously alongside the animal to keep his path straight for the contestant. The start is ruined by a 10-second penalty if the horse releases a fraction of a second too soon. The steer must clear to a certain predetermined point before the horse can be released. The start is an explosion of speed triggered by the flip of the contestant's hand while releasing the tension on the reins. The dangers are imminent. Either leg could snap in a heartbeat. The contestant must not miss the mark and land up over the head of the animal. The contestant wears no more protective gear than a cowboy hat and a pair of jeans. Most steer wrestlers are big, beefy ex-football players. Many top-ranked bulldoggers are former NCAA All-American linemen. Sid Steiner was considered too small to find any success in his chosen event.

At nineteen, Sid Steiner entered professional rodeo. Sid threw his first steer in 1995 and bought his tour card, or rodeo permit, the same year. For the next eight years, Sid Steiner rose through the ranks methodically with an unyielding work ethic and the determination to settle for nothing less than a world championship. Along the way, if a few feathers got ruffled, all the better. Rodeo had its first long-haired, tattooed, pierced, Eminem-listening, Kid Rock–jammin', bad-ass, world champion celebrity. With a colorful family heritage dating back more than a century, the Steiner legacy continued to flourish when Sid Steiner capped the 2002 rodeo season with a title. While *The New York Times* and *USA Today* have called professional rodeo the next NASCAR, many in the nation scratched their heads as millions rode the growing rodeo tidal wave. Americans were looking for things American, and rodeo was all red, white, and blue. Combining the growing popularity of America's first extreme sport with a young man that was bringing an entirely new audience into the fold created a phenomenon.

At the National Finals Rodeo when a world champion is crowned, the champion will take a victory lap around the arena aboard a speeding quarter horse. PRCA rules dictate that all contestants wear a cowboy hat and a long-sleeve, collared shirt during all events within the arena. At the 2002 NFR, when Sid Steiner won the world championship, the sold-out arena waited as Sid mounted his horse behind the chutes. The newly crowned champion exploded from the bowels of the stadium waving his competition shirt, exposing massive, tattooed arms and wearing only a cut-off T-shirt. The crowd erupted as Sid pulled his horse to a stop in front of the lower-level box seats and pulled out a gold medallion necklace caught beneath his shirt. Sid tapped the medallion worn around his neck and threw his fist in the air. The medallion was a gift to Sid from 11-year-old McKenna Galbreath, who had been very sick and was given the medallion by an Irish priest. Galbreath's wish had been to attend the NFR in person and meet Sid Steiner. Sid was able to spend some time with her prior to the eighth round.

Bobby Steiner sat behind the steer wrestler's box during the 10th round and watched as his youngest son won a world title. Bobby Steiner had won the World Bull Riding Championship in 1973. The year 2002 was ending in spectacular fashion. Bobby's oldest son, Shane, had reached the top of the Billboard charts for RCA Records with his hit song, "What If She's an Angel." Tommy Shane Steiner had appeared in concert at the Orleans Hotel in

Las Vegas on the last two nights of the 2002 NFR. Sid introduced Shane at the Orleans on Friday, December 13. On Sunday, December 15, Sid wrapped up the second world championship in the Steiner family with a spectacular run to open the 10th round. Bobby had been banned from the family seating cluster for most of the Finals because he was too nervous, and, therefore, became less than an amicable viewing partner. Bobby calmed down enough before the final round to rejoin the family. While waiting for Sid to take his victory lap, Bobby thought back to when Sid was a young boy growing up in Austin. Amidst the thundering crowd at the Thomas and Mack Center, a father smiled.

During the grade school years, the Steiners lived on a ranch located on the shores of Lake Austin, outside the Austin city limits. Bobby had used his father's address in Austin for schools. The boys had to be driven into town each day and dropped off at their grandfather's house. They rode bikes to school from there each day. Tommy Steiner was Bobby's father and the boys' grandfather. Thomas Casper Steiner was forever Teece or T.C. to everyone in the family.

When Sid was in the fourth grade, he came back to Teece's house one day to find his father waiting to drive the boys back to the ranch. Sid's mother, Joleen, usually picked up the boys in Austin each day. Sid told his father that some sixth-grade boys were going to be coming over. Sid had received eight stitches above his eye from a four-wheeler accident earlier in the week. Within minutes, a group of not less than 10 sixth-grade boys pulled up on bikes to the driveway at Tommy Steiner's house. Bobby remained quiet as he observed his youngest son. There were no requests for assistance. Bobby asked no questions concerning the origin or escalation of the dispute. Sid walked outside. Bobby and Shane followed.

Bobby peered at the older boys and announced one rule. "You can cross this driveway one at a time. I won't interfere." Bobby looked at his son. "What about those stitches?"

"I'll be fine," Sid answered, again requesting no assistance from his father or his brother.

The first kid eagerly stepped off his bicycle and approached Sid. Of course, the first boy was supposed to be the toughest one in the group. Bobby questioned the wisdom of his noninvolvement when the 12-year-old boy, who crossed his driveway to beat up his 10-year-old son, seemed to be all too confident. Preteens had always been tough in Texas, and Bobby wondered if his independent tough love was about to fail miserably.

Sid didn't wait for any formal instructions. Sid Steiner sent a fourth-grade fist into a sixth-grade mouth. The sixth grader was overwhelmed. The older boy fell to the ground in a heap, and Sid pounced on top of him and pulled the boy's shirt over his head. A flurry of Steiner fists made that distinctive, queasy crunch upon finding their fleshy target. Bobby always told the boys that no matter how big your opponent was, they were all the same size on the ground. The fight lasted no more than 30 seconds. Not another boy dared to cross that driveway. Bobby had to pull Sid off the sixth grader and help him back to his bike.

Shane, a fifth grader at the time, watched and smiled. Bobby knew Shane stood poised and anxious to jump in and assist his younger brother. Best friends and brothers are normally two separate issues with young boys. The Steiner boys enjoyed a bevy of friends at school, but the selection of a best friend was a decision that Sid and Shane never addressed. They were each other's best friends. Sid wanted to handle the problem alone. The Steiner boys were never rewarded for doing the right thing. The boys were expected to do the right thing. A Code of the West was not an enigma to the Steiner family. The code was always about respect and ethics.

\*     \*     \*

Sid continued to circle the arena floor. This was not your father's rodeo. Bobby laughed at the shirt-waving display following the championship. Sid would join the family in minutes on the main concourse, just as he had each night of the Finals. Bobby Steiner excused himself for a moment.

Sid's wife, Jamie, is a gorgeous little blond and a world-class barrel racer. The former Jamie Richards from Kennewick, Washington, qualified for the 2000 NFR, winning one round. After the awards ceremony on Sunday, Jamie and Sid were running to the limousine parked outside the Thomas and Mack Center. The events of the day were still a blur. Jamie jumped in the back seat of the limousine. One reporter caught up with Sid before he could get into the vehicle. A bevy of reporters appeared instantaneously. Sid Steiner explained that he had to go, but thanked everyone for all the attention during the season.

"My wife is waiting." Sid smiled and pointed to the rear seat of the limousine.

"How is marriage, Sid?" a reporter for *ProRodeo Sports News* asked.

"Marriage is great, boys. Jamie and I have so much in common," Sid replied.

"Like what?" the reporter persisted.

"We're both crazy about me!" Sid smiled jokingly and jumped in the limousine.

In the days following the 2002 NFR, Commissioner Steve Hatchell of the Professional Rodeo Cowboys Association would field numerous complaints to the PRCA headquarters in Colorado Springs. The complaints were regarding Mr. Steiner's lack of deference to the long-standing rules concerning apparel. When queried about the rule infractions by

Sid Steiner at the 2002 Finals, Commissioner Hatchell responded with, "What infractions?"

Commissioner Steve Hatchell came to the PRCA from a New York executive search firm, hired six years prior to bring new guidance and leadership to the association. Hatchell was the former president of the Big Eight Conference and the former executive director of the Orange Bowl in Miami. Hatchell's background was Division I NCAA athletics. Under Hatchell's direction for the past five years, professional rodeo's popularity and visibility across the nation has exploded. When asked about Sid Steiner's impact on professional rodeo, Hatchell was emphatic: "Sid Steiner's impact on the sport of rodeo has been immeasurable. The life blood of any sport is young people. For any sport to survive and thrive, young fans must be drawn to the core of the competition: the competitors. Sid Steiner has been an adrenaline injection to the sport of rodeo. Sid likes to stretch some long-standing rules within the PRCA, but he seems to know just when to stop. We are all drawn, at times, to the eccentric. We are always drawn to the best. When the best brings eccentricity to the game, we all become fans."

—James Pomerantz

# Creating an Image

Let me start by saying that I am a vain person. I mean, I really do care how I look. That's something I don't think most guys would admit, but what the hell, we might as well tell the truth here. I can remember picking my clothes out the night before school in the fifth grade. Shane was the exact opposite. Mom would just throw him whatever she grabbed, and he would wear it—not me though. I had an image to keep. I was also a big fan of the saying: look good, feel good, do good.

When I first started to rodeo, I pretty much played by the rules. By that, I mean looking like a PRCA cowboy was supposed to look. The longer I rodeoed, the more I saw how everyone looked alike. I had always looked up to the Brian Bosworths, the Jim McMahons, and the Dennis Rodmans of the world. After going to rodeos for a while, I began to feel like a sellout. I wasn't being true to myself. I was wearing this stuff because I felt like I had to, not because I wanted to. So, after a while, I decided I was going to be myself at all costs. I knew a lot of people wouldn't like it, and I would be talked about, but hey, any publicity is good publicity, I thought.

Gradually, I started to wear wilder shirts, wild boots, and then wild pants. The wilder my clothes got, the more people started paying attention. I even started to listen to the music I really liked: rock 'n' roll and rap. I remember this new guy had an album out that mixed both kinds of music. Maybe you've heard of him—Kid Rock? I bought his album in Salinas, California, one day and I was sitting around my truck digging my new CD. A bunch of guys came over and couldn't believe what I was listening to. I told them this was Kid Rock. They sat and listened and began to think this was some pretty good stuff. After a few songs I told those guys this Kid Rock is one bad-ass dude. Shit, they ought to call me Sid Rock. Everyone cracked up laughing and went to telling everybody. The nickname was started as a joke, but caught on quickly and stuck. I have to say I always did like that name.

At the Finals in 2000, I fully transformed myself into the role of Sid Rock. Did I mention I always loved to play dress up? It was the perfect opportunity to dress like a rock star and kick some ass at the rodeo. Contrary to what a lot

Nobody ever disputed the fact that I was a real cowboy, it's just that I never really looked the part. (Photo courtesy of Mike Copeman Photography)

of people thought, though, I would never trade substance for style. What I mean is that I didn't just want to look good, I wanted to do good looking good. The two had to go hand in hand. If I had not done well in the 2000 Finals, I would have been a joke, but I did do well. I placed in seven of ten go-rounds, won the third go-round, and got out of there with $43,000. Not bad for a rock star playing rodeo, huh?

Needless to say, not everyone loved Sid Rock. The PRCA received its share of hate mail on me. People were saying that I was not what rodeo was all about and they should do something about me. Some old cowboys even called some of the judges at the Finals and told them to screw me around. (Like I needed any help from those guys.) I thought it was great though—creating a controversy, that is. I remember telling reporters, when they asked about the commotion, that I'm not for everybody to love, but somebody will love me. The hype got even bigger when I appeared on the cover of the *ProRodeo Sports News*, the publication of the PRCA, with no shirt and a red fur coat. It sounds like a fashion faux pas, but it really turned out pretty good. I was pictured standing with my dog, Bosworth. The caption read, "Waddup, Dawg?" People were pissed; they threatened to cancel their subscriptions if they ever saw me on that magazine again. I never told Bosworth though; I figured it would hurt his feelings. He has always been so proud of that picture.

**So, after a while, I decided I was going to be myself at all costs. I knew a lot of people wouldn't like it, and I would be talked about, but hey, any publicity is good publicity, I thought.**

I signed on with Wrangler that spring. As far as sponsorships go, Wrangler has been one of the big dogs of rodeo. To be honest though, they were the last deal I wanted to go with. I was the edgy cowboy with the wild clothes. Shit, I was Sid Rock. I always figured they would just tone me down, but in the negotiations, they told me Wrangler wanted to tap into a new generation, a younger generation, generation X. They said they wanted me on board to help style this new line of clothing called 20Xtreme. This would be a takeoff of their 20X line that they had for a while. So let me get this straight: I'm going to have my own line of clothes and some greenbacks to put in my pocket? How much better could this be? I was going to be the cowboy that made Wrangler hip and mainstream. Now let me tell you future athletes out there to always get these things in writing. Every time I made suggestions on wilder, hipper clothes, they were just swept under the rug. The only way I could figure out to look edgy was to wear all black. Now I don't know if you have ever been to Nampa, Idaho, in midsummer, but it's extremely hot, especially if you're wearing black. I fried my ass off that summer trying to look cool. It crossed my mind at one time to just drop the ego and put on the bulldogger plaid shirts. I just chalked those thoughts up to a mild heat stroke and stayed with the black.

We found out Jamie was pregnant that summer and decided to head home until next year. By the time 2002 rolled around, Sid Rock was ready to make a splash again. Fortunately, things went well and I was headed back to the Finals in 2002. I couldn't wait. Sid Rock loves Las Vegas. I was determined not only to look good, but to win a world title. I sent all of my Wranglers to Trish Townsend, my brother's stylist, and told her to make them look wild. I had met one of my favorite actors, Mickey Rourke, in Los Angeles, while getting a tattoo. (That's another long story I won't get into.) He had some jeans on that had been cut up and had some material added on the legs to make bell-bottoms. They looked cool as hell so I told Townsend to do that to mine. My wardrobe turned out great and so did the Finals. I was ecstatic to win that world title for a lot of obvious reasons, but one reason was to let all the critics know that I wasn't all about my look; turns out Sid Rock was a cowboy too.

# 2

# The Family Lineage

Before indoor plumbing, automobiles, airplanes, and Thomas Casper Steiner, Buck was born. Buck Steiner began a three-century life a few miles east of Austin in Cedar Creek, Texas, on December 2, 1899. Buck's reign did not end until May 2001. Buck Steiner was my great-grandfather.

Buck never enjoyed what we consider a formal education. He always told me he had a high-third-grade education. At six years old, he could pick more cotton than any 10-year-old in the county. He learned the cowboy ways at an early age and grew up hard and mean. Drafted into World War I, Buck was denied actual entry to the armed forces because of a severely broken leg from a bull riding accident. Buck survived by breaking horses for 50 cents a day.

Buck had leveraged enough money to start his own construction business in the early twenties. After hard times in Texas claimed the 17 homes under construction that he was overseeing, he turned to the American creed of supply and demand. Bankruptcy in Texas was not an option. When the banks called in their loans, foreclosure and restitution were the only options. Buck, a big man at well over 6' tall and 200 pounds, had lost his first battle. He was broke and owed banks from Austin to Houston. Buck began selling whiskey.

Over the years, Buck developed a lasting friendship with Frank Hammer. Hammer was a Texas Ranger and the one associated with the relentless pursuit and capture of Bonnie and Clyde. Buck's relationship with Hammer opened many doors in the turbulent times of the Texas twenties. Through those open doors, he drove the trucks loaded with illegal liquor. Buck's Austin connections gave him the access to the governor's mansion, and my great-grandfather catered many of the lavish parties. New relationships through those parties bore new business opportunities. Buck amassed four warehouses in Austin over a five-year period during the twenties. The warehouses were used solely for the storage and distribution of illegal beer and spirits. The sheriff's department was paid to keep its distance. Parties at the State Capitol and the surrounding political residences were all catered by Buck Steiner. He partnered with Benny Binion, the hotel and casino founder. During those days in Texas, Binion covered the Fort Worth area and Buck handled the Austin area. They were sales distributors, and their territories were to be respected.

Buck hated the label of bootlegger. *Bootlegger* was a term derived from the days of smuggling moonshine in the hollow of a man's boot. Buck was a whiskey broker. The underlings that delivered the alcohol were bootleggers. Men learned quickly not to refer to Buck Steiner as a bootlegger. Buck met with the nation's major distributors on a monthly basis in Miami. Also present at these meetings was Al Capone.

Here's my great-grandfather, Thomas Casper "Buck" Steiner, pictured at age 91, about 10 years before his death in 2001.

Buck always tried to shield the family from his associations. I can recall very little of Buck discussing his days running liquor. The connections could never benefit the members of Buck's family and could only harm them. Buck never spent a day of his life trying to impress anyone.

The whiskey and beer came to Texas on bobtail cattle trucks. The deliveries and transportation of the illegal alcohol were facilitated by the participation of many Texas law enforcement officials. The consumption of alcohol was not considered a felony by most of the adult population. Most Texans consumed alcohol regardless of the law.

Federal attempts to pursue and arrest the bootleggers and brokers proved almost futile. On one occasion, Buck's shipments of whiskey were being tailed through Mississippi by a convoy of federal agents. Rather than risk the potential legal entanglements, Buck and his drivers steered three oversized cattle trucks, loaded with whiskey, into the Mississippi River. The agents stood helpless as the evidence disappeared. The whiskey trade made Buck financially secure.

When the Eighteenth Amendment was repealed in 1933, Buck had eased himself out of the whiskey business and into the land business. He also started a rodeo company named the Steiner Rodeo Company. In the years following prohibition, Buck was most likely the only man to describe Al Capone as a really nice guy and great fun to be with. Buck was never indicted for any crimes.

Buck and Viola Strosser, a beautiful brunette, married in 1920. We always called my great-grandmother "Mamoo." Buck and Mamoo had two children. Myrtle Irene was born in 1921. Thomas Casper Steiner Jr. was born in 1926. My grandfather's initials were T.C., and we called him Teece. Teece entered the air force at age 17 in 1944. Myrtle Irene was killed in an apartment fire in South Carolina. She was 22 at the time of her death and married to a serviceman. Buck never got over Myrtle Irene's death. It just made him harder. Buck and Mamoo separated when Teece was 15 because of Buck's infidelity. They remained separated for more that 40 years without a divorce. Buck always took financial care of Mamoo and had regrets until the day he died about the way he treated her. There were always questions about

Buck married Viola Strosser, whom we all called "Mamoo."

why the pair never formally divorced. Mamoo could have achieved financial independence in a divorce settlement with Buck. As the years passed, Buck kept Mamoo on an allowance and always made certain her financial needs were met, but he called the shots.

When Teece left for the air force, Mamoo was devastated. Her marriage collapsed, her daughter had died, and her son was leaving for the military, all within two years. She looked at her son just before he left for military service and asked what she should do.

"When I get back from the air force, I want everything to be just the same as I left it," Teece stated.

"You know," Mamoo said years later, "I just never asked again."

Buck ran for Travis County sheriff in Austin during the Depression. Although he garnered little support, Buck was a colorful candidate. Clad with twin .45 caliber, pearl-handled pistols, Buck campaigned, oblivious to the reservations of the voters. Even in Texas, skepticism followed political candidates packing pistols. At the Nighthawk Restaurant in Austin, Buck was asked to remove the weapons while in the restaurant. He ignored the request of the restaurant owner. Persisting with his sidearms, Buck exclaimed, "Goddamn, boys, have you seen the election returns? A guy with no more friends than I have better carry guns with him!"

**In the years following prohibition, Buck was most likely the only man to describe Al Capone as a really nice guy and great fun to be with. Buck was never indicted for any crimes.**

In the thirties Buck opened Capital Saddlery. The shop was located in downtown Austin, three blocks from the State Capitol. Capital Saddlery made custom saddles, boots, luggage, and assorted leather goods. The Lavaca

Street location was an old firehouse. Renovated over the years, the saddle shop became known for quality products, employing more than 50 boot- and saddle-makers at any given time. Capital Saddlery supplied all the saddles and boots for the Sears and Roebuck catalogs, as well as the Montgomery Ward catalogs. The saddle shop became home for Buck. A recluse, he lived in a single room on the ground floor of the saddle shop for more than 50 years. The room had a single bed, a small refrigerator, and one tiny bathroom. He had amassed a fortune in land and lived like he was broke. Money was never anything to be enjoyed by Buck. Money could be hoarded, but not enjoyed. Buck vowed never to go broke again after the construction debacle.

Land deals grew in size with each year. The early Steiner Ranch emerged below Mansfield Dam on Lake Austin. Sixty-five hundred acres were purchased in Bastrop, Texas, some 30 miles east of Austin. Buck grew wealthier and meaner. He once buried one hundred thousand dollars in cash to avoid detection by the IRS. The money was put in coffee cans and buried on the Bastrop ranch. When the money was retrieved, Buck realized he hadn't taken into consideration the effects of decomposition. The bills had virtually disintegrated over time. My grandfather, Teece, was able to bring the bills to a Treasury Department office for verification and was reimbursed for

$85,000. Buck's only comment was that the federal government had screwed him out of fifteen grand.

Buck owned apartment buildings in Austin during the forties. He once tossed a tenant out for filling his apartment with whores. The tenant had not heeded the repeated requests to cease. The man's name was John Overton. Overton and his brothers had formed a little gang. The Overton Gang robbed banks. They vowed to kill Buck. Buck put up a sign in the window of Capital Saddlery inviting the Overtons to stop in for a visit anytime. They never came. Some wondered silently. Some

**Persisting with his sidearms, Buck exclaimed, "Goddamn, boys, have you seen the election returns? A guy with no more friends than I have better carry guns with him!"**

knew. Buck was that mean. Even mean people cringed when the subject turned to my great-grandfather.

The Steiner Rodeo Company was growing as well. Buck started it as a wild west show. Buck, as the front man for the rodeo company, was a nightmare to deal with. Teece was summoned by Buck to take over the business after Teece left the service. Teece wanted to go to college, but Buck insisted that he return to Austin and help with the businesses. Buck told his son that he was dying and did not know how much longer he would live.

Teece was as friendly as his father was mean. Teece was tall, athletic, and handsome. When Teece left the air force, he abandoned his dreams of law school to help Buck in his dying years. Teece didn't know that Buck's dying years would last more than half a century. In fact, Buck outlived Teece. Teece was well-suited to run the rodeo company. The established accounts welcomed his demeanor with open arms after years of dealing with Buck. Teece was an accomplished rodeo contestant. He rode bulls and bareback horses, but cut his competition days short to focus on the rodeo company.

Teece was a man who knew what he wanted, but also knew the right way to get it—unlike his father, who would stop at nothing to get what he wanted. One incident happened in 1958 when the Steiner Rodeo Company was contracted to produce a major rodeo in Cuba. The rodeo took place just weeks before Castro took over the country. The rodeo animals were sent to Havana by ship, and the cowboys and our family flew over. The rodeo spanned more than a month, but with the turmoil in the country, the crowds were not what was expected. After the rodeo, Teece sent his family, the rodeo contestants, and the personnel to the airports for the flight home. He went alone to collect his contracted money, knowing something could go wrong. The government paid Teece $50,000 in cash that was put in a brown paper bag. (Today, that would be like running around a foreign country with half a million dollars in cash.) The Cuban government had a cab waiting to take Teece to the airport. The cab driver drove around in circles for almost an hour. Teece knew something was wrong and reached in his pocket, opened his knife, and put it to the throat of the cab driver. Teece always laughed when he told that story and said it was amazing how fast the driver's sense of direction came back. Sometimes even the kindest people have to do what it takes to get by.

My grandparents: Beverly Bunton Steiner, who was always "Mimi" to us, and Thomas Casper "Teece" Steiner Jr.

Teece met Beverly Bunton of Marfa, Texas, at the University of Texas in Austin. We called my grandmother "Mimi." Teece was not a student, but had been introduced to Mimi, a Longhorn student, by friends. They married and had three boys, Bill, Bobby (my dad), and Blake. Teece let the boys grow up within the traveling Steiner Rodeo Company. They had traveling tutors and learned to ride as a way of life. Bill and Blake ran into trouble with drugs and the law. Teece was always there; however, he gave the boys enough rope to succeed or enough to hang themselves. Dad followed his dream to the rodeo arena with a world championship buckle in bull riding at the age of 22.

Dad told me a story that gives one unique perspective on Buck. Many years ago, a young man entered the saddle shop with what appeared to be his parents. Buck was around 50 years old at the time. That would have made the year around 1950. The young

**Teece knew something was wrong and reached in his pocket, opened his knife, and put it to the throat of the cab driver. Teece always laughed when he told that story and said it was amazing how fast the driver's sense of direction came back. Sometimes even the kindest people have to do what it takes to get by.**

Buck (left) with Beverly, Teece, and their three boys, from left, Bobby (my dad), Blake, and Bill.

man voiced his displeasure over some work done on his boots. Buck didn't care for the man's attitude and told him to leave. Words continued and Buck invited the man outside to settle the issues. Buck proceeded to knock the man to the ground in a one-punch altercation. The young man's father came running out to defend his son and Buck dropped the father just as quickly. To Buck's surprise, the mother came running out screaming hysterically at Buck. Without the slightest hesitation, Buck dropped the mother as well. Buck could be a little rough around the edges.

By 1973 Mom and Dad had their first son, my older brother Shane. Dad walked away from rodeo as a bull rider immediately after winning the world title when Shane was two months old. Teece had offered Dad a full partnership in the rodeo company.

Mimi and Teece were both great people and loved by all. Teece could be a tough man, as all Steiners have proven to be, but he was an emotional man as well, not afraid to embrace his children. My father always smiles when he recalls his parents. Everyone said that Mimi was a drop-dead double for Elizabeth Taylor in her prime. She was a statuesque beauty until the day she died in 1989 of lung cancer.

Teece inherited Buck's hard-nosed determination, but paired it with a heart the size of Texas. Dad got the best from both of them. I am an emotional person, and we are the product of what came before us. Dad was a fighter and taught us to stand up for ourselves. The first time I watched Dad fight, things took on a new dimension. I was 12 years old, and Mom threw a birthday party for Dad at a location near the Austin ranch. One of my Uncle Blake's friends got out of hand and offended some of the guests. The man professed to be an ex-marine and didn't appreciate Dad suggesting that he tone it down. Finally, the guy called Dad out. Dad did not hesitate to accommodate the request and when the disturbance became physical, Dad broke the guy's nose with a right hand that must have felt like a jackhammer. That punch left a mess! Needless to say, anything that Dad told me to do from that day forward was done a little quicker and with a bit more enthusiasm.

Buck was never a family man like Teece. When Shane and I were small, we would run to hug our grandfather whenever we went to visit him. Buck was respected, but we kept our distance. Buck enjoyed hearing about any fights that we experienced. Buck took an unusual liking to me and referred to me as "Tuffy." Teece passed away in September 1999. Buck died in May 2001. The legacy of the Steiner name in Texas was born with Buck, but bore lasting roots with Teece, and continues today with my father. I attribute my disposition to Teece and my temper to Buck. I can only reluctantly acknowledge small memories of pride from the depths of poverty that Buck conquered. I once thought that Buck was a great person, but it turns out that I never really knew the man.

# 3

# The NFR, Round One, 2002

Rodeo has always been a series of goals to me. Achieve one, and then move on to the next. When I first got my tour card, my goal was not to embarrass myself. Please, just let me get out of the chute without missing my steer completely!

With the first taste of prize money, you start thinking about filling your card. When that time comes, you are cool! Man, things don't get any better than that. The rodeos start to get a little bigger, the money creeps up the ladder, and the crowds start getting bigger. You make some good runs in practice and you start telling yourself that four seconds flat would have won a couple of rodeos that you have already competed in. Now you know that you have the talent. It's just a matter of doing it when it counts.

Finally, you win that first buckle. Shit! First place! I don't care if the rodeo was in Tupelo, Mississippi, or Bend, Oregon. You have arrived in your own mind. From that point on, you are hooked and you either get good or you die trying. I left "good" somewhere back in 2000. When you make it to the National Finals Rodeo, you find out what you are made of. Making the NFR became the measure of my year. If I didn't make the NFR, then I had a shit year. Nobody remembers who finishes 16th. Man, from the time

There's no atmosphere like the one at the NFR, and I sure didn't go there in 2002 to finish in 15th place. (Photo courtesy of Mike Copeman Photography)

you throw your first steer at Denver you are thinking about the Finals. After 2000, making the Finals was not good enough. Winning a world championship became an obsession. While the top 15 competitors in each event make the NFR, I didn't want to make the NFR as the 15th guy. Making the NFR is like a sprint: you don't want to run to the line, you want to run through the line.

I was a competitor before anything else in rodeo. I didn't wish bad things to happen to any other bulldogger, but I wanted better things to happen to me. If I was in a position to win and there were two guys left with a chance to beat me, did I hope they screwed up? You're damn right. I hoped they broke a barrier or got a steer that ran too hard. I pulled for my friends to finish second, but I never put anyone ahead of myself.

When the final round was over at the Cow Palace in San Francisco, there were guys screaming for joy and there were guys crying because they just got knocked out of the NFR. I had a good summer in 2002. My last rodeo was in Waco, Texas, in early October. I finished in the money at Waco, and by the time I left for home, I was in fifth place in the world standings. From there, it was more important for me to go home, practice, and relax. I rodeoed hard all summer, and if I fell a spot or two, it was worth it to me for the time off. I knew there was no way I could have gone to Las Vegas with the lead. I knew that I had to win it at the NFR. My mindset was all-important to me. I wanted to be around my family and the ranch in Bastrop. I wanted to give my horses time to get fresh, and I needed time to get fresh. The ranch was what I needed. Going in seventh or eighth was fine with me, and that's what I did. I took a couple of months to develop a plan to win the world championship.

During October and November, I practiced hard and trained hard. I ran, lifted weights, and stretched every day. I would throw between eight and ten steers a day. As the Finals got closer, I started running fewer steers until I got to one steer a day. I wanted to replicate the conditions in Las Vegas exactly. I called Butch Kirby, a PRCA official and good friend of the family, and got the exact measurements for the arena, the box, and the chute. We groomed the Bastrop practice arena meticulously. Too many injuries occur when guys practice on bad dirt. We blocked off the arena at the ranch to the exact measurement of the Vegas arena. Then I started running one steer a day because I wanted to get used to knowing this was the only chance I had all day. When you run a bunch of steers each day, your mind tells you that it's all right to mess one up because you have plenty more coming. I had to lose that mindset. If I had a bad run, then I wanted to think about it until the next run. I got my mind to treat the practice run as the real thing. I had my hazer, Alfalfa Fedderson, come down from

Oklahoma to practice with me. Not only was Alf my hazer, he was a good friend and we had a blast traveling together. I had lights installed so if we had to, we could practice at night. Bryan Fields, a great friend and fellow NFR qualifier, and I would build a fire next to the arena. The ranch hands would bring down a cooler of beer, and when we earned the right to stop, we'd sit by the fire and drink beer and talk about the runs. I loved those nights and those practice runs. The more people around, the better I practiced.

> **Making the NFR is like a sprint: you don't want to run to the line, you want to run through the line.**

I worried some about losing an edge going into the 2002 Finals. In 2000, when I made the Finals, I had to rodeo all during the fall and I was winning. I went into Las Vegas on a roll and I was sharp. In 2002 I took the two months to prepare for the Finals. It had been two months since I had won a dollar. Practice can only bring you so far. The competitive tension of a big rodeo, the crowd and the adrenaline, cannot be manufactured in practice. There was nothing I could do about it by the time the Finals rolled around. The first round was so important. Would the juices be flowing so that I would be able to perform at a higher level, or would they mess with my head?

A trip to the Finals is the most exciting trip in the world to pack for. You basically move to Las Vegas for two weeks. It's the neatest feeling to pack and know what is ahead of you. You will never have a closer group than the guys you made the Finals with. Only they know how hard I worked to get to the Finals, and I know how hard they worked to get to the same spot. Not everyone was that close during the year. You were competing against each other, and everyone was in and out of the rodeos pretty fast. As the year progressed, you were thinking more about your rank than how to make new friends. The first couple of days in Las Vegas were the time to relax and party with the guys that left everything out on the road to get to this point. It's like 15 brothers hanging out together.

**The first round was so important. Would the juices be flowing so that I would be able to perform at a higher level, or would they mess with my head?**

The night we got our NFR contestant jackets was cool. I rented a stretch Hummer limousine to pick everybody up to go to the NFR jacket presentation. I remember Bob Lummus' face when he jumped into that limousine. Bob and I didn't get a chance to hang out much during the year, but on this night we were best friends. My wife Jamie and a whole crew of steer wrestlers traveled with me in the

Hummer, and we partied all night. We all knew that we had all day Thursday to lose the hangover. The Finals began on Friday. Here's a 30-seat Hummer limousine filled with a bunch of liquor and a bunch of cowboys acting like little kids. I told them all, "Man, we are all friends tonight. Enjoy tonight, it's my treat, but it's every man for himself come Friday night." I'll never forget that night.

We unpacked at the Orleans Hotel. My brother, Shane, was booked for a concert at the Orleans on the following Friday and Saturday. The staff at the Orleans was great to my family. I got six or seven rooms on the same floor. I wanted familiar people around me. I wanted my group: positive people. I didn't want anything negative around me. I didn't want to wake up and walk out my door and see some numbnuts in plaid shorts or some overweight Tommy Bahama on his first trip to Vegas screaming about the $125 jackpot he had just won. When we pulled into Las Vegas on Monday night, it was exciting to see a huge billboard featuring Shane and me. A good friend of the family, Tony Spears, owns a billboard company and came up with the plan to put us on one of his billboards. How cool was that?

> "Man, we are all friends tonight. Enjoy tonight, it's my treat, but it's every man for himself come Friday night." I'll never forget that night.

It took hours for me to get the horses settled at the arena. I wanted to walk them after the long trip. They were my lifelines as a bulldogger. The horses were stalled behind the Thomas and Mack Center in separate stalls. I brought both my bulldogging horses, Slim Shady and Boss. I had planned on riding Shady, but was forced to get on Boss because of a practice pen injury to Shady.

Jamie and I settled into the hotel with our one-year-old daughter, Steely. Changing the living environment of a one-year-old can be intense. I brought a humidifier because the air in Las Vegas was too dry. I didn't want to take any chance on any of us getting sick. The mattress wasn't comfortable to me or anyone else that I talked to, so I bought some foam padding to place on top. I was meticulous about every aspect of my mental and physical health. In 2000 when I made the NFR, I figured that was the end of my rodeo career so I partied every night. Las Vegas is a hard place for me to sleep. I remember in 2000, I'd go to bed at 4:00 or 5:00 in the morning and wake up at 8:00. I'd walk down to the lobby café, try to force some food down, and the casino bells were going ding, ding, ding, ding. The perf (that's rodeo slang for the evening's performance or competition) started at 6:30, and I would arrive at the arena well ahead of that time. I remembered a few times arriving at the Thomas and Mack in a fog.

In 2000, I was content to make the Finals and just have a good time. But two years later, I was in a completely different mindset. I was almost obsessed with winning the world championship. (Photo courtesy of Mike Copeman Photography)

I was determined not to repeat the mistakes I made during my first trip to the Finals in 2000. I know that the best thing that happened to me in 2002 was going out on Wednesday night in the limo with my bulldogging buddies. I got as drunk as I could and it took me all day Thursday to start to feel human again. I remember looking at the clock at 6:30 Thursday evening and trying to imagine running a steer the way I felt. I said to myself, "Screw this shit!" I don't know what difference two years had made, but I found out quickly that I couldn't drink like I used to and recover as quickly. Thursday night I just had a couple of beers at the Gold Coast, shot the shit with everyone, and tried to relax. Jamie and I went back to the room and ordered dinner from room service. Some guys set themselves up to let their minds control their actions. If I went out early, had dinner, and then went directly back to the room, I would have way too much time to think about the next round. The NFR was a privilege. My dad told me to always stay focused but enjoy the experience. A return visit is never guaranteed. Plus, for me, I knew that I wasn't going to rodeo for many more years, so I definitely took advantage of the good time. I didn't stay out until 4:00 in the morning each night like I did in 2000, but we went out each night in 2002 with friends, had a few beers, and relaxed. That was time that I was not thinking about the next round.

> **I was determined not to repeat the mistakes I made during my first trip to the Finals in 2000.**

Cowboys tend to get superstitious at the Finals. Some guys are really superstitious all the time. I'm not. My dad had a hot dog before the first perf on Friday night. He rarely eats hot dogs because he is such a health nut, but he was just hungry at the time. Friday night I placed third, so Dad had a hot dog every night before each round. It just about made him barf, but the routine was the important thing.

Cowboys somehow relate success to the events surrounding the competition. We all know the damn hot dog had nothing to do with my run, but if the run went bad and Dad didn't have that dog, then he'd be kicking himself in the ass for not making the sacrifice. After the Finals, Dad told me that he would never eat another hot dog as long as he lived. Cowboys have never staked a claim to the world's most forward-thinking groups, but we are what we are.

I prepared for each night of the Finals the same way. At 4:30 P.M., I would get in the shower at a normal temperature. I would shampoo and soap up like any other day, but as I was done, I turned the shower to as cold as it would get. My football number in high school was 22. Standing under the cold water, I would count to 22, then scream, "You can't beat me now!" I'd be throwing punches into the air and screaming, "Come on, MF. Try to beat this SOB now!"

Jamie would pin my number on my back and I'd get into the limo. I had a limo every night thanks to my good friend Charlie Horky. Hork Dog owns CLS Transportation, one of the largest limo services in the country. My driver's name was Lucky. I'd listen to some Kid Rock or some Eminem on the way to the perf. Lucky would start moving his head to the music, and he'd start yelling, "You're ready now, man. You are ready now!" Lucky's voice would get gradually louder and the music level would rise. We were rockin' by the time we got to the Thomas and Mack.

Every time I arrived at the Thomas and Mack, I felt like I was running late. I called Frank Thompson each night while I was in the limo. Frank is a true friend plus a great bulldogger, and I valued his advice more than he will ever know. I would get out of the limo and run to where my horses were. I might have been an hour early, but for some reason, I always felt like I was late. I always saddled my own horse because I am very picky about my pad and saddle. I wanted the tension exact and I had to do it. I would get my horse saddled up and then let my trailer driver, Whiplash, warm him up. About 15 minutes before the round, I had Whip lope Boss to the left. Boss had a tendency to run too close to the steers and loping him to the left seemed to help. The tension mounted. When I arrived at the Finals, I could swear there was a smell in the air. Adrenaline causes an aroma. My nostrils were five times their normal size and everyone was pumped. I bounced everywhere. There was a spring in my step. Sometimes I wondered if I looked like Richard Simmons or something.

I went to the Justin Sports Medicine room before every round. I took advantage of being stretched out and having my ankles taped. This is how I imagined a pampered athlete was treated. They had Red Bull in there, and I would grab a couple of Red Bulls. They were free, and I remember Buck always telling me to take advantage of free stuff. I wanted my ankles taped. I'd get stretched. I liked feeling like I was about to play in the Super Bowl. Most of the guys in the Justin room were roughstock riders who had been beat to shit the night before. We would all wish each other luck and talk about the previous night's ride. It kept my mind off my run.

I'd fire up with my second Red Bull and get hopped up for the Grand Entry. Horses feel how nervous you are. On Thursday night the practice run for the Grand Entry went without a hitch. On Friday night, when everyone was nervous as hell, the horses sensed it. There was always a bunch of horses rearing up. A few of the roughstock riders got tossed. It was hilarious. World-class rodeo contestants were getting tossed like kids at a county fair. A few of the rough-stock guys were not used to riding nervous saddle horses.

**The tension mounted. When I arrived at the Finals, I could swear there was a smell in the air. Adrenaline causes an aroma. My nostrils were five times their normal size and everyone was pumped. I bounced everywhere. There was a spring in my step. Sometimes I wondered if I looked like Richard Simmons or something.**

The Grand Entry was run each night before the round began. The contestants from each state were introduced as the states were shuffled into the arena in alphabetical order.

My brother's stylist helped me with my clothes in Las Vegas. Trish Townsend dresses many artists in country music. I had her fly down to Vegas for the NFR. Townsend was always edgy with her hairstyles, but I was limited because I had a contract with Wrangler and I had to wear Wrangler. She put together the whole wardrobe and I would wear what I felt like on any given night. In 2000, on the night we got our contestant jackets, I showed up wearing a red fur coat and leather pants. On the second night in 2000 I wore a shirt my mom had found. It looked like a feathered leopard skin, certainly made for a lounge singer. No one could believe that I was actually going to wear that shirt in competition.

"Steiner!" some of the other contestants exclaimed, "you're not going to wear that f***ing thing, are you?"

"F***in'-A right I am!"

That night I wore the shirt to show everyone that Sid Steiner had made the NFR, and I could wear whatever I wanted. My steer ran like a deer that night. I had to chase that son of a bitch halfway across the arena floor and barely caught him. I finally got my hands on his head and managed to get his ass on the ground in what seemed like an eternity. I am certain that the steer caught a glimpse of my shirt as I left the box and ran as fast as he could away from whatever in the hell was chasing him. After my run, I pulled that shirt off, balled it up, and threw it into an alley behind the Thomas and Mack. I'm sure there is some Las Vegas pimp wearing that shirt to this day.

I knew Mom and Dad were out there and wearing that shirt was a way to acknowledge them. Dad opened a few eyes when he competed. Officials had threatened him on many occasions that he would be booted from various rodeos if he wore some outrageous clothes or didn't cut his hair. I knew Mom and Dad were smiling. That was the only time that I was nervous about what I wore. Even for me, that was a bit out there.

The steers are drawn about an hour before the perf. Some guys will go down and take a look at their steer. I normally don't do that. After you run enough steers, you can sometimes tell which steers are going to run hard. Some droop their heads in the pens, and others are upright and very aware of their surroundings. It's not exact, so I stay away from that. I don't want to form an opinion about an animal that may not be accurate. I got the steer, and I'd find out soon enough. There are three different sets of steers. Each set of steers number 15. For the first three nights, the steers were all different. After the third round, we had seen them all. Alfalfa's wife, Kelly, videotaped them all. So from the fourth round on, we would watch the tape of the steer I had drawn. I watched the steer maybe eight to ten times. I watched his tendencies. If he went left out of the gate, Alfalfa and I would plan accordingly. We videotaped the steers because I was never very good at remembering them. Some guys remember every steer they ever threw. I had trouble remembering my practice steers. I might have asked someone about steer number 20. They would say, "Dude, you had that steer last week!" Shit, I didn't remember, and that was something that I should have been better at. Anyway, these steers had not been to a rodeo for two months. Some of them could have gotten bigger. It was all still a crapshoot.

The first round arrived. I was up seventh. My mind was racing. No one remembers second place. There are no gold buckles for second place. I didn't want second place. I had really stepped in it. Here I am with an entire entourage, being driven to the arena in a limo, styled to the max by a stylist for the stars, skating to the edge of unconventionality, and taking the heat from die-hard "keep-everything-old-school" cowboys. I had to be good, and nothing but first place was going to do it. I didn't want to be the guy that tried to make a splash with his "look" and not his talent.

I hadn't been to a rodeo for more than two months. My heart was pounding like a jackhammer. My favorite horse, Slim Shady, was hurt. Now I was on Boss, my backup horse. That fact seemed to swirl in my head moments before the run: I'm in the biggest rodeo of my life and I'm not on my best horse. Boss was great at most places, but never was wild about small buildings. Right then I caught myself thinking of the reasons why I wouldn't win. I refused to allow the negative thoughts to control me. I pulled myself together and decided to rely on the hard work and preparation that I had done. I reminded myself of the conversation I had with Steve Duhon, three-time world champion steer

**There are no gold buckles for second place.**

wrestler, the night before. Dad and I were walking through the casino of the Orleans Hotel when we ran into him. Steve was one of the greatest steer wrestlers of all time and, without a doubt, the toughest. Not only did Steve reassure me that Boss would work great, but my confidence soared when he announced in front of a large crowd that I was his pick to win the world title. There is nothing like a compliment from the very best.

Some guys can't watch the runs ahead of them. I like to watch the other guys go. I imagine myself in the saddle with one hand on the reins and the other hand on the saddle horn. I release the reins as the steer runs. (I also like to imagine I can remember the steers, but I can't.) If they make a good run, then I think, great! They just got the crowd going for me. Now, watch what I can do. Two guys before my run, I get on my horse and close my eyes. I always try to visualize a perfect run. One more run, then me. My stomach knots up. The rodeo announcer's voice is booming through the arena. I hear nothing. I'm up. Alf and I move into position. Boss is calm in the box. My horse releases from my hand. Boom! I threw the steer in 4.1 seconds and took third for the round. It was worth maybe $8,000, but more importantly, I felt good. My horse worked well. Boss came through. I knew at that point that even if Shady didn't get sound, I would be fine with Boss.

We all went out each night after the round. Jamie and I had friends come in each night and my family was there. I didn't plan on getting messed up each night, but again, too much time in the room is too much time to think about things that can go wrong. Some guys just take it way too seriously. They create their own demons and fight them alone each night while trying to stay away from the temptations of Las Vegas. I tried to relax and enjoy my friends without going nuts. Four or twelve beers later and I was fine.

# 4

# Establishing Grit

My dad grew up in the rodeo business. Mimi and Teece, my grandmother and grandfather, had been running the Steiner Rodeo Company for several years when my dad was born in 1951. My grandparents had a home in Austin, but they traveled constantly. Mimi's parents were also a ranching family in West Texas. My dad and his brothers spent many summers there.

Rodeo was a way of life for nearly 11 months a year for my dad. Mimi and Teece took their sons on the road with them from almost the time they were born. School was an afterthought. There were some years that Dad went to traditional Austin schools and other years when he was homeschooled or tutored on the road. Dad told me that long before Willie Nelson made the line famous, his heroes had always been cowboys.

Teece could have excelled as a rodeo contestant, but he chose to focus on running the Steiner Rodeo Company. By the time my dad was born, most of the company's rodeo clients were begging Teece to leave Buck at home. Many people felt that Teece could have been a great bareback bronc rider, but he was happy to take over the tremendous responsibility of producing rodeos across the country. The Steiner Rodeo Company was the first rodeo company to bring the sport to many locations east of the Mississippi River. Atlanta, Indiana, Kentucky, and Tennessee were some of the new venues hosting rodeos during the mid-fifties. Truckloads of livestock, bucking horses, parade horses, steers, calves, bulls, tack trailers, chutes, pens, and specialty acts were regularly hauled cross-country. Mimi and Teece took their boys everywhere.

Dad grew up worshiping the bull riders. Of course, Dad had a unique opportunity to get to know all of them. He figured out how to study the bulls. He knew every tendency and odd quirk associated with every bull in the company pen. The bull riders went to Dad when he was still quite young to seek clues to the particular bull they had drawn for the rodeo perf. My dad was drawn to the bull riders. He started riding the roping calves at age five. As an exhibition before the rodeos began, my dad and his brother would ride the calves. They graduated to the bull-dogging steers at age seven. Junior rodeos entered the picture soon after. My uncle Bill was a better bull rider than Dad in those early years. Bill and Dad regularly placed first and second at junior rodeos. Dad knew from the get-go that he wanted to be a bull rider. The bull riders had always been the coolest guys on the circuit to my dad. He told me long ago that their influence and the danger had everything to do with his choice of events. Dad told me that bull riders were also the laziest cowboys. There were no

**The Steiner Rodeo Company was the first rodeo company to bring the sport to many locations east of the Mississippi River.**

regular jobs, there was no punching a clock, and the only thing you had to carry was a rigging bag. That was right up his alley.

Dad got on his first bull at age 11. The bull weighed about one thousand pounds. The addiction was complete. Full-grown bulls entered the picture at age 13. Dad rode some of the bulls owned by our rodeo company as a junior; he then rode them as full-grown stock in the National Finals a few years later.

At 16, Dad entered a rodeo in Jackson, Mississippi. The ride was short, but Dad hung out with the bull riders for the rodeo. He was on his own and his path was set. My dad flew back to Austin the next day and went back to school. He

After growing up around the Steiner Rodeo Company, my dad left school halfway through the 10ᵗʰ grade to follow his dream of being a bull rider. (Photo courtesy of Burton Wilson)

signed every paper handed out during the day and never read one of them. After school, he went home and wrote a note to Mimi and Teece. Dad left home to ride bulls. He had a permit at 15 and his card at 16. My dad left school in the middle of the 10ᵗʰ grade. He went to stay in Dallas with a friend and they set out to follow their dreams. Most of the weeks were spent working odd jobs to earn the entry fees.

After a few weeks had passed, Dad entered a Steiner Rodeo and he saw Mimi and Teece. My grandmother used to slip him a $100 bill. She never told my grandfather, and my dad never argued or refused the help. That first year on the road, Dad began to travel with three other cowboys that had all been to the Finals. His confidence grew. Dad started winning good prize money at the start of the next year. He placed in Denver, placed in Amarillo, and won a go-round in Fort Worth.

Dad made the Finals in 1970 at age 18. The touring cowboys believed that Dad was too young to do anything at the Finals. The bull-riding event was not a kid's game.

Now the Finals had a bell-bottomed hippie wearing puffy shirts and sporting long hair and a mustache. Most cowboys sported the military, boot camp haircut and the traditional plaid shirts. No one had facial hair. My dad showed up to most of the rodeos blasting Humble Pie and Black Sabbath. He told me that he never even liked most of that music. He listened to it because it made him different and he stood out. Who says we are not our fathers' children? Making it to the NFR was a fluke, but they thought the Finals would knock the flower child back to Earth.

Looks like my grandfather, Teece, has some words of wisdom for my dad before a competition. They said Teece could've been a great rodeo competitor, but he focused instead on operating the business side of the Steiner Rodeo Company.

The first round that year, Dad drew a bull that had never been ridden. That is, until Dad rode him. Dad won the first and third go-round. After the sixth round, Gary Leffew and my dad were tied in the lead for the NFR. Leffew won the title, but my dad had earned the respect of his peers and the respect that comes from within. David Glover, another top bull rider, proved to have a profound effect on Dad's career. Glover was instrumental in giving Dad the confidence to rise to that final level of competition while performing beyond his own expectations. That kind of composure and self-reliance eluded many rodeo competitors for their entire careers. Dad found it at 18. Making the Finals came first, but failure at the Finals often became one's worst enemy. The more years that a cowboy made it to the Finals, the greater the pressure to win the world championship.

**Dad told me that bull riders were also the laziest cowboys. There were no regular jobs, there was no punching a clock, and the only thing you had to carry was a rigging bag. That was right up his alley.**

In 1973 Dad won the Cow Palace and entered the Finals in first place. Donnie Gay and Larry Mahan were second and third. Dad rode nine out of ten bulls at the Finals and won the title. A misconception about rodeo revolves around the dollars associated with the sport. In 1973 Dad won a total of $29,000 for the year. The average major league baseball player's salary that year was $32,000. The average National Football League player's salary was $35,000. The gap was there, but small. ABC *Wide World of Sports* carried the Finals in 1973. Today, a world champion in rodeo may earn close to $200,000 for the year with a good Finals. The average MLB player's salary exceeds two million dollars. Today, the gap is like the Grand Canyon.

James Caan interviewed Dad on *Wide World of Sports* after he won the 1973 world bull riding title. The questions got around to what was next. My dad retired right there. At age 22, a world championship buckle in hand, Dad retired from competition. After a relatively brief career, that was it. Dad never received the major injuries associated with bull riders. Sure, there were the broken wrists and arms and even a broken collarbone, but never a season-ending catastrophe or a life-threatening scare. Dad always said that he knew when to hang and when to fly. This had nothing to do with jumping off; it had to do with knowing when you're fixing to take one. That sense of your impending demise was something that few had. The time came when everyone decided not to tempt fate forever. Some found it earlier. Dad had nothing more to prove.

Injuries often had nothing to do with talent. Dad often returned to the example of Lane Frost. Frost could ride a

By the age of 22, Bobby Steiner was the best bull rider on the face of the planet.
He promptly retired from competition after winning the 1973 world championship.

bull as well as anyone he ever saw, and he was killed in 1989 at Cheyenne.

Dad told us that he knew too much about the bulls and the event. As kids, we were not going to grow up to be bull riders. Of course, as small children, that was exactly what we wanted to do. There was another factor that led Dad to keep Shane and me away from the bulls. There were always unusually high expectations associated with a son entering the same field as his father, especially when the father excelled in that field. Marvin Shoulders was a great cowboy, but never won a world championship. Marvin Shoulders was compared constantly to his father, Jim Shoulders, and took unfair heat for not winning the world championship. Jim Shoulders won 16 world championships and was rodeo's first phenomenon. Marvin Shoulders won plenty and rode great, but to some it wasn't enough. Dad did not want that for us.

Travel was another reason that my parents had no burning desire to push Shane and me into rodeo. When the decision was made to marry the sport of rodeo, then you could kiss your family good-bye. You had to be gone nine to ten months a year if you wanted to be good at it. Dad wasn't ready to watch his family leave home. As it turned out, Shane became a singer, and I became a steer wrestler, and we both left home anyway.

When Shane and I were small, we always pictured ourselves following in Dad's footsteps. Man, we wanted to be bull riders. Dad finally took us out to ride some calves. We had a rodeo arena on the ranch. They used it mainly to buck out horses and bulls. Dad put on bull riding schools after he retired and was well-respected as a coach and teacher of the sport. Dad never got us any bull ropes or gloves because he didn't want to encourage bull riding. So when he took us out to the arena to ride the calves, we were surprised and pumped up. This was it! We were going to be bull riders! We used some rubber dishwashing gloves Mom had and some flank ropes for our bull ropes. Dad told us that we needed to ride as many times as we could that day.

Remember, Dad never encouraged Shane or me to pursue rodeo competition. We were encouraged to pursue every other sport outside of rodeo. Naturally, we wanted to be like Dad. Shane went first that one day we were allowed to be bull riders. I remember Shane looking up at Dad and asking what he should do. Dad, the former world champion in the event and a respected coach for young riders, looked down at his oldest son and said, "Hang on." Shit, he told me the same thing! Hang on? A former world champion bull rider was watching his two young sons ride for the first time, and the only advice he coughed up was hang on. Where were the directions to ride up high above the animal's shoulders, balance with your free hand, don't lean back, and keep your chin tucked? Just: "hang on!" That's all Dad told us. We got knocked around good. Dad wasn't interested in how we did. He wanted us to get beat up so we would never want to do that again. "Keep riding, boys," I remember him saying that day. "Ride as many times as you want to today because this is the last day you are going to ride these animals." That was it. I didn't think about rodeo again

That's me at four years old, trying to follow in my dad's footsteps.

until I was almost 19 years old. I was five and Shane was six on the day we rode our last calf.

Mom and Dad met at a rodeo—where else? Mom was a barrel racer. Joleen Hurst was from Fort Supply, Oklahoma. Fort Supply is in the panhandle of the state and at that time had a whopping population of close to three hundred. Mom grew up on a farm approximately seven miles out of town. Mom was the new hot girl on tour. The cowboys used to talk about her, and Dad told me that they all agreed that Mom had the nicest backside they had seen. I am discussing my mother, so you will forgive me for not elaborating on the subject of rodeo cowboys leering at the woman who raised me. Mom and Dad both went to the Finals for the first time in 1970, and they both finished eighth. They started dating in 1971, and that year they both finished third at the Finals. They got married 11 months later in the summer of 1972. Mom was 19 and Dad was 20. In 1973 Dad won the world championship.

When Dad retired from competition, he started helping run the rodeo company full time. The travel was still there, but we all went with him. My mom always traveled with Dad, and they brought Shane and me whenever we were not in school. When we got to school age, things changed. Mom and Dad were determined to give us some type of normal life. We were sent to schools in Austin, and we were encouraged to play all sports, especially baseball and football. Mom and Dad were gone often when Shane and I first started school. When it came time for Mom and Dad to leave with the rodeo company again, the results were the same. Shane and I cried, and Mom cried too. Dad often had to drag Mom away from the house. The time had come to make a change. When an offer came in to buy the rodeo company, Teece asked my father what he wanted to do. Dad knew the chance might not come again. The Steiner Rodeo Company was sold in 1981. Dad became a full-time father and coach. Mom had a full-time job keeping us out of trouble.

> **I remember Shane looking up at Dad and asking what he should do. Dad, the former world champion in the event and a respected coach for young riders, looked down at his oldest son and said, "Hang on."**

Our family lived on Lake Austin when we were kids. We owned more than five thousand acres west of the Austin city limits. The property backed up to Lake Austin. There was a full-size baseball diamond built near the house as soon as we were old enough to play ball. Dad drilled us every day. He would ask if we were flunking anything in school. If the answer was no, then it was outside to practice sports. If the answer was yes, Dad told us to try harder

55664

in school, then it was outside to practice sports. School was an athletic venue to me from an early age.

Mom brought more tenacity to our family than most men I knew. When I was 10 years old, Mom was at one of my little league games. She never missed a game. During the game, another mother from the other team began heckling me. "Steiner can't hit!! Throw strikes!" Mom asked the woman to stop. The heckling continued, and Mom ran over to the other side and tackled the woman, slamming her to the ground. Word got around fast: it was best not to mess with the Steiner boys. Mom wasn't born a Steiner, but she was sure made for the Steiner family.

I don't think I could talk about Mom's tenacity without talking about Fort Worth and a trip to the stockyards. I was 19 and had just started my rodeo career. Mom and Dad were going to Fort Worth for a bull sale at the stockyards. I took a friend, Jason Hollen, and we were going to make a cool weekend out of the trip. I knew some girls going to college in Stephenville, and we agreed to meet at Billy Bob's Texas, one of the largest nightclubs in the United States.

We arrived at the club and got settled in. Then Jason and I went to find the girls we had planned to meet. It seems the girls had been there for a while, and some of their college boyfriends were there with them. When we got to their table, the guys took an immediate dislike to us. One thing led to another, and I ended up being the centerpiece in a bar fight. It didn't take the bouncers long to show up, and I still don't think they were there to break up the fight. They wanted to become part of the action.

In these situations, the guy on top usually gets hit the hardest, and that just happened to be me. I was also lucky enough to flip the big, raging bouncer to the floor, not knowing who he was. There were 10 bouncers that joined the dislike-Sid-Steiner party. They soon got me under control, with my hands pinned behind me in handcuffs

My mom and dad, Joleen and Bobby. Mom may not have been born a Steiner, but she sure did fit into the family tradition of sticking up for each other no matter what.

and my clothes and hair firmly gripped in the bouncer's hands. We proceeded to the administration offices.

Now it didn't surprise me when from out of nowhere, Dad became part of the action. I then somehow found myself back on top, with no hands. I looked down and saw my mom tangled in the feet of the big bouncer that she had just tackled. That was about as good as things got for the rest of that fiasco. We got out of there that night just about the time I think Mom started to enjoy herself.

To the bouncers from Billy Bob's: hey, it was fun while it lasted. Maybe we can do it again sometime. My place this time, not yours, and I promise not to bring my mom.

I have become an extension of the values that my mother and father instilled in me. Does that make me any less of an individual? I feel it has made me even stronger. I am very proud of those values, and I hope my own children will follow my lead. Right and wrong are very black and white to me. I don't tolerate rudeness, and I choose not to ignore it either. I'll respect you and what's yours, but when I am not afforded the same, then I will not walk away. I am my father's son.

# 5

# The NFR, Round Two, 2002

The morning after the first round, I woke up early and tried to go back to sleep, but couldn't. I had stopped working out about two weeks before the Finals to avoid being tight. I stretched every day. The most exercise in my day was a free massage every day at the Gold Coast and a few 12-ounce curls at night. The massage took about an hour each day. Whip checked my horses every morning—except for the morning he got blind drunk and didn't show up at all. I'd usually get to the Thomas and Mack around noon and hand-walk the horses myself. Everybody was out doing the same thing.

All the contestants wished each other well and talked about the previous round. No one knew the steers on the second night, so we were all in the same boat. Normally, I did not stay long after the horses were walked. I had autograph sessions to attend for Wrangler. I knew I was up fifth on the second night. The steer was the mystery. We would not see the entire run of steers until after the third round.

The world champion is determined by the total money won during the year plus the money won during the Finals. The top 15 on the money list of the world standings went to the NFR. In 2002 the leading money winner during the regular tour stops was Cash Myers, with $88,139. The 15th-place finisher was Ivon Nelson, with $59,361. Less than $30,000 separated the entire field of 15 steer wrestlers going to the Finals. I finished the year in seventh place going into the Finals. I had won just over $74,000.

The Finals present the most possible money to win during the entire year. The notion that whoever would win the world championship had to win the title at the NFR was never more evident than in the 2002 steer wrestling standings. No one had the lead locked up, and no one even had a sizeable lead. The field was wide open. The money at the Finals was substantial. Each go-round paid $13,923 for first place, $11,003 for second, $8,309 for third, $5,839 for fourth, $3,593 for fifth, and $2,246 for sixth. The total score for the 10 rounds in the Finals is another big payday possibility. The average title paid an additional $35,705 for first, $28,968 for second, $22,905 for third, $16,842 for fourth, $12,126 for fifth, $8,758 for sixth, $6,063 for seventh, and $3,368 for eighth. Each round was unbelievably important.

If anyone claimed that they did not watch the standings in the first few rounds, they were lying. My stomach was in knots during the afternoon before a perf. In the morning I'd eat a couple of eggs and some bacon, but by the afternoon I couldn't eat anymore. Some days I tried to force down a banana just to get something in my stomach. Two guys ahead of me in the standings missed their steers in the first round. The standings presented some unique match-ups. I tried not to analyze the possibilities, but most of us were guilty of trying to look ahead.

I had plenty of support during Finals time in Las Vegas, but having my family there was the most important. That's my wife, Jamie, on the left, my mom and dad, my brother Shane, and our good friend Butch Stokes.

Any of the 15 bulldoggers in the 2002 NFR could have won the world championship. Each man had more than enough talent and desire. So much of what we do is out of our control (like the draw). Don't get me wrong: everyone has to pay their dues and make the sacrifices that allow them to join an exclusive club. But there is always a bit of karma involved.

**Any of the 15 bulldoggers in the 2002 NFR could have won the world championship. Each man had more than enough talent and desire.**

Cash Myers came to the 2002 NFR in first place. Rodeo has been Cash's life. Butch Myers, Cash's father, was a past world champion steer wrestler. Cash's older brother, Rope, won the 2001 world championship. Cash definitely had a shot to win the world championship in 2002. He is a tremendously talented bulldogger. The Myers team was smart and well equipped.

Bill Pace entered the Finals in second place. It had taken him 10 years to make the Finals. Injuries tried to end Pace's NFR dreams, but he was all about winning. He was so excited to be at the NFR. Bill Pace was one of the guys that I wanted to make the NFR with. I knew he would do well at the Finals. It was sometimes hard to know where you stood with Pace, but after the 10th round, I found out what a good friend he was to me, and still is.

Joey Bell came into the Finals in third place. He was always a good cowboy. I felt that he was fortunate to travel with Cash Myers and always had good horses and a good crew. The Myers boys know how to rodeo and it rubbed off. Joey Bell was from New Jersey, and I frankly didn't put him at the top of my concern list.

Bob Lummus came into the Finals in fourth place. Bob is a great guy! He is a big country boy with the best attitude I've ever seen. If you don't like Bob Lummus, then I don't like you. Bob was a streaky competitor, but his mindset could handle a few mishaps. If he got on a roll, then I knew he would be hard to beat.

K. C. Jones entered the Finals in fifth place. Jones is a rodeo lifer and a great cowboy. He loved the rodeo life, and 2002 was his first NFR. I worried more about the guys that had been to the NFR before, but Jones had the character to excel in Las Vegas.

Rod Lyman came into the NFR in sixth place. Lyman is a big cowboy from Montana. The program said 235 pounds, but he's a biscuit away from 270. He had been to the NFR 15 times and hadn't won a title. That monkey can grow on your back as the years go on. The pressure was great enough at the Finals. The added pressure of not winning for so many years has stifled even the best bulldoggers. I knew Lyman would be good for a couple of go-round wins, but I thought that a missed steer might knock him out of the average race.

I came into the Finals in seventh place. If anyone thought that I got to where I was because my family had the resources to help me, then screw them. I practiced harder than anyone I had ever worked with, traveled with, or heard about.

Luke Branquinho entered the Finals in eighth place. He is a terrific guy. Everyone called Branquinho the Kid or Fatty, but we knew he was a great bulldogger. He had a real shot to win the world championship, and I looked at him as a direct challenge to my title hopes.

Birch Neggard rode into the Finals in ninth place. He was another terrific steer wrestler. I knew he would be tough to beat. Neggard wins go-rounds and is always up there in the average hunt. If it hadn't been for one really bad steer, he would have been right there.

Lee Graves was in 10th place to start the Finals. The Canadian champion had earned the respect of his American competitors. Graves had been to the Finals five times, but I didn't foresee him winning.

Curtis Cassidy entered 11th. He was not a concern. He eventually missed four steers and finished 15th in the average.

Bryan Fields is one of my best friends in rodeo. He came into the Finals in 12th place. We all call him Sleepy because he never got too fired up about good things or bad things. I know Sleepy and his wife, Cindi, very well. He and I practiced together all the time, and we knew each other's strengths and weaknesses. Fields was a top contender to take the world championship.

Jason Lahr came into the Finals ranked number 13. Lahr is a good friend. He has a similar background to me because he came from a family with money. He never had to win rodeos to stay afloat, but he did anyway. Lahr worked his ass off to make the Finals. People tend to think anyone

**If anyone thought that I got to where I was because my family had the resources to help me, then screw them. I practiced harder than anyone I had ever worked with, traveled with, or heard about.**

with money has it made. The negative talk follows you everywhere: "He's just in it for a good party," or "I wish I didn't have to win every week to stay alive." People bad-mouth you for having money, then hit you up for help. They ride your horses and don't want to pay mount money because they think you don't need it. People find out that you are interested in their horse or rig, and they jack the price up ten grand because it's you. Some don't feel the need to chip in for fuel or offer to pay for a plane ride. Hell, it's better to have the opportunities, but the position carries some baggage. Lahr always handled it well. I never apologized for my family or my opportunities, and neither did he.

Todd Suhn earned his ninth NFR at spot number 14. Suhn could have won it. With the right steers, there is no question about his talent. As far as just being a cowboy goes, in my opinion, he is the best.

> **I was not feeling my oats or looking to bust out and shout it to anyone, but I really felt like I was the one to beat.**

Ivon Nelson was the gunner in 15th place. I did not know Nelson well at all. He did not present my main challenge.

A missed steer could cost you the title. Most of us figured that if you were not at least third in the average, then the world championship would be awfully tough to win. I felt good about the first round. I had placed third with a 4.1. I had a good frame of mind going. I was not feeling my oats or looking to bust out and shout it to anyone, but I really felt like I was the one to beat. If a contestant isn't confident, then he should hang it up and go home. The NFR setup is perfect for a guy who throws fast steers. I like to catch them quick. The Thomas and Mack Center was a great setup for me. The building was small and the runs were very short. I didn't get a great steer on my second run, but I caught him quickly enough and placed fifth with a 4.4. My horse, Boss, worked well again, and I needed to stay right up there for the average title. You aren't going to win every go-round or have a shot at every go-round. Sometimes, you have to take what the steer gives.

I grew up with a world champion for a dad. That always made me proud. I wanted that for my children. What I did on those 10 nights would have a lifelong effect on my family and everyone I loved. I didn't go to Las Vegas in 2002 to have a party every night. I was there to win!

# 6

# Steiners, Schools, and Sports

Mom truly had a difficult time leaving Shane and me at home before the rodeo company was sold. The travel was actually fun when Shane and I were very young. Dad let us ride ponies all over the rodeo grounds, and we'd hang out with the cowboys all day long. At five and six years old, things couldn't get much better.

I remember one particular rodeo in Big Springs, Texas. I was five and Shane was six. We had a Shetland pony that Dad would drag along to every rodeo for us to ride. He always allowed us to ride the pony in the Grand Entry. We would follow directly behind Dad, who led the parade of horses. Before the Grand Entry in Big Springs that year, all the rodeo cowboys took me aside to instruct me on how to show that

That's my dad and me in 1976. I was into sports ever since I can remember, and from the looks of it, I guess I was always a 'horns fan.

the Steiner Rodeo Company was number one. When the entry began, I followed Dad into the arena. Dad was always proud to have his sons ride into the arena with him. On this particular night, the crowd began going nuts. Dad looked into the stands and couldn't figure out why the crowd was reacting so boisterously. Finally, Dad turned around and looked at me. Well, I was riding my Shetland pony proudly, my arm raised high, and my middle finger extended rigidly into the air. I was flipping the bird to the entire crowd! The cowboys had explained to me that the middle finger salute would show everyone that the Steiners were number one. The salute had to be raised during the entire ride around the arena. They told me not to let my arm fall during the entry. Shit, I was so happy that they included me in their loop I would have believed anything. And I did!

Shane and I were good students during most of elementary school and middle school. I had the ability to get along with all of my teachers. Even if I couldn't stand a particular teacher, I figured they were easier to deal with when they liked me. Shane shut down when he didn't like a teacher. Our jobs were to pass the courses and not receive one failing grade. Beyond that, Shane and I had no parental pressure to excel in school. Pressure came to excel in athletics and that was just fine with me.

Baseball, soccer, and waterskiing became the focus of my youth. We took to baseball pretty fast. Dad loved practicing with us, and that love for practice paid off in so many other sports for me. Shane and I made all-stars in baseball for a few years. One of my baseball coaches told my dad that he should get us into Pop Warner football. Dad said no. He did not want us playing football until we were in the seventh grade. After some serious prodding, Dad relented and allowed us to join Pop Warner football at the age of eight. Before our first practice, Dad gave the speech I still remember.

The family that plays together stays together. Here's my dad, Shane, and me ready for action.

"Boys," he began, "when a Volkswagen Beetle runs into a Suburban, the results can surprise you, especially when the Volkswagen Beetle is moving much faster than the Suburban. The VW can knock the big Suburban off the road because the VW has superior speed." After that speech, I was going to make certain that I was that VW.

We jumped out of the truck all pumped up and headed for our first football practice. I loved the hitting drills. I didn't know shit about positions or formations, but I knew that I liked to deliver the hits. At one of the first team meetings, the coach requested a middle linebacker. He said that the middle linebacker position was the team tough guy. The middle linebacker had to take most of the hits and he would be expected to make most of the tackles. I nearly jumped out of my pants. I screamed, "I'm your middle linebacker!"

I played four years of Pop Warner at fullback and middle linebacker. Football was what I lived for. In Pop Warner, everyone was about the same size. When I got to junior high, the other kids had started growing and I hadn't. It didn't matter too much then because of the football background I had received in Pop Warner. My last year of Pop Warner, our team won third in the state of Texas. I had some basic football skills and would be damned if a little size would prevent me from kicking ass in junior high as well.

When I got to high school, I was at Lake Travis. I played quarterback and middle linebacker. The coach sucked. The team sucked. Winning wasn't a big priority, and that bothered me. After four games, I knew that I had certain goals that couldn't be achieved at Lake Travis. I wasn't very big, but I wanted to excel in football. Dad saw the frustration and fury in my eyes every day. He asked me if I wanted to change schools for a better coach and a better football foundation. Dad's former football coach, Jim Acker, was the head coach at Anderson High in Austin. My girlfriend was going to Anderson and most of the kids I went to grade school with attended Anderson. We could use my grandfather's address and get right in. Hell, there was no decision to make.

**At one of the first team meetings, the coach requested a middle linebacker. He said that the middle linebacker position was the team tough guy. The middle linebacker had to take most of the hits and he would be expected to make most of the tackles. I nearly jumped out of my pants. I screamed, "I'm your middle linebacker!"**

Coach Acker had coached Dad in the ninth grade, and he welcomed us with open arms. At Lake Travis, the senior football players made life hell for the freshmen. I don't just mean some light hazing. They messed with the younger kids until they had them scared to death. They left Shane and me alone for the most part, but I watched them torture some other kids. They did some mean shit, like when the seniors pissed in someone's Listerine bottle and laughed at some timid freshman when he took a mouthful. I was all too happy to get out of Lake Travis. The one good thing to come out of Lake Travis was Chris Cokins, who is still one of my best friends. When Shane and I arrived at Anderson, all of the senior players shook our hands and took us out to lunch. They told us that if we needed anything to let them know. I was in heaven.

The transfer from one high school to another had absolutely nothing to do with academics. Dad didn't like the way the football coach at Lake Travis handled his boys and he got us the hell out of there. Dad wanted his sons to be smart to the ways of the world above being smart to the ways of the book. Buck made it to the third grade. Teece made it to 10th grade, and Dad made it to the 11th grade. I was the second Steiner to graduate from high school. None of my uncles graduated high school. Sports were everything to my dad and to us. Academically, we had to pass. I seriously believe that if the state of Texas did not have a no-pass, no-play policy, Shane and I would not have even attended school. Of course, we never would have missed a game.

My freshman year at Anderson, I played cornerback. I was small and I came into the team during the year so I played wherever they wanted me to play. I made some good hits during the year and started to develop a reputation for hitting. I played some tailback, but defense was where I excelled. That summer, Dad sent us to a football camp in California. My brother and I lived on a college campus for one week and did nothing but football drills, games, scrimmages, and technique training. Hall of Fame players Howie Long and Ronnie Lott were among the coaches. Ronnie Lott was my idol. I was playing defensive back at the time, and Lott hit like a freight train with eyes. The camp was in San Bernardino, California. I soaked up everything Ronnie Lott had to say. I watched him walk because I wanted to walk like him. I watched him talk because I wanted to talk like him. The camp came before my sophomore year.

That fall, Anderson fired coach Acker and I was devastated. Coach Acker knew my game, he trusted me, and he had confidence in me. He knew how good a player I was. They hired a new coach and told the players that if we saw a big guy walking through the halls that looked like he played defensive tackle for the University of Texas, that was our new coach. Coach Ray Dowdy turned out to be the best thing that happened to my high school athletic career.

Coach Dowdy's first speech to our team at the start of my sophomore year had a profound effect on me. He looked at the team and began to pace the room. Coach Dowdy announced that he had a theory on this football team.

"My theory is this," Coach barked. "F*** you, f*** your mom, and f*** your dad. If you don't like anything about me, or the football program that I will lay out, then you can get the f*** out of here right f***ing now! This school has had a pussy reputation for some rich boys trying to act like

That's me on the Lake Travis eighth-grade team on the left, and as an Anderson High freshman on the right—after a much-welcomed change of schools.

football players. Not on my f***ing watch. If you don't play your asses off, then trust me, I'll make you f***ing leave this team."

I couldn't believe it. I had known this coach for less than five minutes, and he had used the F-word seven times. I loved this guy. I had a pretty good junior varsity year. I wasn't big enough to make the varsity as a sophomore. During my sophomore year, most of our best players went up to varsity. My goal was to showcase what I could do. Our team sucked because the better players weren't playing junior varsity. Coach Dowdy liked me and respected my headhunter instincts. I loved special teams, defense, or anything that involved hitting. Two weeks before my junior year, coach Dowdy called me into his office and announced that I was going to be varsity middle linebacker. Coach Dowdy told me that I was his toughest player and it was time to make the move. He asked me if I could handle the job. I told him in no uncertain terms that I could absolutely f***ing handle the job! I believe that I might have skipped the profanity, but I was so excited it might have squirted out.

Coach Dowdy played for the Chicago Bears and was an All-American at the University of Texas. Coach had done everything I dreamt about doing. My junior year, Anderson High School won one game. That didn't matter to me. I had Friday night fever and I had it bad. If it hadn't

been for football, I'm certain that I never would have finished high school. Football was everything to me. I knew that
I wanted to play college football. My senior year, I got up to
approximately 180 pounds. I
thought that I had to be at least
200 pounds to get some attention from the major colleges.

On my first senior weigh-in
day, I went out to lunch in
Austin and drank 15 glasses of
water. I had two five-pound
weights strapped inside my
jock strap. When I got on the

**I couldn't believe it. I had known this coach for less than five minutes, and he had used the F-word seven times. I loved this guy.**

scale, my weight was 208 pounds. Coach Dowdy yelled,
"Good f***ing job, Steiner, I knew you could do it." I jumped
down from the scales and almost killed myself running to
the bathroom. In the Anderson football program, there I
was, Sid Steiner, middle linebacker, 208 pounds.

One great asset that any good linebacker needs is a killer
defensive lineman in front of him. My senior year it was Ben
Fricke, a mountain of a kid in high school, and a kick-ass
lineman. Ben was all-state in high school and wound up
playing for the Dallas Cowboys for three years. During our
first game, Ben ate up the offensive line and I was free to hit
everyone. It was like stealing. Then my defensive wrecking
ball broke his neck. There went my free reign.

The season went well in spite of Ben's injury. Anderson had their best record in 20 years. I received interest letters from Iowa State University, Southwest Texas State University (now known as Texas State University–San Marcos), Brigham Young University, and Texas Christian University. I was thinking this was the deal. I felt that Southwest Texas, a Division II school, was my best option. I didn't have the grades to attend most major Division I schools.

During my senior year, I had to skate out of an algebra course because the teacher couldn't guarantee me a passing grade. My coach talked to him and I talked to him. At first the teacher told us that as long as I put forth an honest effort, he would pass me. If I flunked, then I wouldn't be eligible for football. On my first test I got a 40 percent. My teacher's name was Mr. Beaver. I'll skip any cheap cracks about his name. The guy endured enough of that without my contributions. I went right in to Mr. Beaver's office and asked him if the deal was still on. He told me that if I continued to score at the current level, he could not guarantee a passing grade. That was all I needed to hear. I dropped that class so fast that I don't think that Mr. Beaver had finished his sentence. I immediately enrolled in fundamentals of math. There was no way I was failing out that year. That sealed my fate to attend a junior college.

For the last game of the year in 1992, Anderson played the third best team in the state. We had the lead near the end of the game. They were punting to us, and all we had to do was run out the clock. They punted, and we were flagged for too many men on the field. They got the ball back, scored, and won the game. We were literally crying on the field. I had security guards come up to me and tell us that was the greatest high school game they had ever seen. I was voted to the all-district team at middle linebacker in 1993, the year that I graduated high school.

As No. 22, I was never the biggest guy on the field, but you'd have had a hard time finding anyone who hit harder than I did.

High school was great for me. I was the one guy at Anderson you wanted to know. I had the parties. I had access to the kegs, and my place was perfect for congregating. Everyone met at the lake house. If we got busted, then I was the one held accountable. I didn't mind. We brought the kegs out and charged for the cups. If we invited kids from a couple of different high schools, then we charged more. We never charged the cute girls. Cups were $4. I always made Chris Cokins work the cup money line. He would charge everyone! I let too many friends slide. We had a nice little enterprise going. If someone was drinking too much, then we insisted that they rally to the tip jar again. If they refused, then we cut them off. If I didn't like someone, I'd charge that person $10 or $15. When that action caused a problem, then we had a fight. A good fight energized me.

Mom and Dad did not facilitate or presume to condone the drinking my friends and I participated in. Dad was not however, naive to the ways of the times. Dad believed that his sons should know what the effects of drinking could be. Dad was a cowboy and always will be a cowboy. Cowboys don't preach. If we were going to drink, then he felt more comfortable when we were on the lake ranch. Dad was concerned about being liable for the kids on the property. I assured Dad that no one would get out on the highway from our ranch. I am not certain that

Shane or I always followed my assurances diligently. By the grace of God, nothing happened involving a serious car wreck or a drunk driving accident.

The parties continued throughout high school, and I grew to be a chronic smart-ass to the police whenever they were summoned. The police would ask where the kegs were. We had already rolled them into the woods as soon as the police pulled down the drive. There was no real way to sneak up on us at the lake ranch. The cops would always approach me, and that fed my sarcasm like gasoline to a fire. I'd huddle my group and call out, "Blue, 31, blue, 31. On two, hut, hut, find the kegs on two, hut, hut."

**High school was great for me. I was the one guy at Anderson you wanted to know. I had the parties.**

Every one of my friends would assume the regular formation of a football play, and then we'd break into a mock play. The results were always the same: big laughs and no kegs turned up. I tried to push the envelope every time. I became the center of attention and I knew the police couldn't do much to me. I wasn't driving and I wasn't in possession of the liquor.

I used to ask the police if they were going to arrest me for being a smart-ass. They called my home on many occasions to provide my father with the details of what a treasure he was raising. Dad didn't go for that act at all. He'd say, "Do what you do and move on. Don't make anyone look bad to amuse yourself." Eventually, even I got tired of my own mouth. Looking back, I'm shocked that not one of the cops took a shot at me just for being an asshole. In Texas, that might have qualified as a justifiable homicide.

**The cops would always approach me, and that fed my sarcasm like gasoline to a fire. I'd huddle my group and call out, "Blue, 31, blue, 31. On two, hut, hut, find the kegs on two, hut, hut."**

I had so many run-ins with the Austin Police Department that I became friends with one of Austin's finest. As we became fairly well known to the Austin police, one officer started showing up frequently to the family home during our parties. His name was Sanford. Officer Sanford was a good man. I apologized to Officer Sanford many times for the crap I dished out as a teenager. The last time I ran into Officer Sanford was after I had returned from three months on the road. I was getting better known on the circuit, but it was a grind. Teece was inducted into the Pro Rodeo Hall of Fame while I was away. My family threw a big-ass party for Teece at his Austin home. Of course, the neighbors called the police, just as they had done so many times when I was throwing a party at Teece's house. Well, Officer Sanford got the call and told me that the sound of that familiar address over the radio brought a tear to his eye. He told me that he was so excited about seeing Sid Steiner that he burned the siren just to get there faster. Sanford was so disappointed to find out that I was away on the rodeo circuit and the party was Teece's.

After my senior season, coach Dowdy called me into his office and told me about a friend he had. Coach Hatch was the head football coach at Ranger Junior College in Ranger, Texas. Coach Dowdy thought that I should go to Ranger. It is located between Fort Worth and Abilene and is approximately three and a half hours from Austin. I looked up to coach Dowdy, and if he thought I should go to Ranger, then I would go to Ranger Junior College and kick some ass on the football field. I signed the papers and assumed that I had a full ride, which meant a full scholarship. When I got there, they told me that I would receive approximately 50 percent of the scholarship due to my financial circumstances. I did not qualify for a full ride because my family did not need the full ride. I was never told that my family's financial standing had anything to do with my football scholarship. I had believed that my ability dictated the scholarship.

All summer, I worked out hard. I was ready to play college football. I had never left home in my life except for the football camp, which lasted exactly one week. I had Shane with me then, so at least I had some connection to home at the camp we attended in California. I was not excited about leaving home for school. About two weeks before practices and school were to start, I told my girlfriend that we needed to take a ride up to Ranger to check it out.

I must preface the upcoming segment on Ranger: I doubt that the following descriptions will turn up in any of the recruiting material used by Ranger in the future. As it turned out, Ranger, Texas, was possibly the biggest shithole of all shitholes that I have ever encountered in my entire life. Ranger, Texas, was just like the West Texas you see in the movies. There were tumbleweeds everywhere. There was no locker room. The football team was expected to dress in the dorms and come to practice in uniform. Ranger was a town where they might have sent convicts to live for some heinous crime. I stood there, shook my head, and said to myself, "What the hell am I doing?"

I met coach Hatch on the same day. I was standing on the field and this guy came up to me and asked who I was. I told him my name and he got very excited.

"Sid Steiner! It's a pleasure to meet you. I thought that you weren't going to arrive until two-a-days started. Hell, I can't wait to get you on the field," coach Hatch announced just after we met.

That guy was hoping that I wouldn't show up until practice started because I would then see what a shithole that place was. I went home and prepared for college. The experience seemed surreal to me at the time. I still wanted to play football and those desires clouded the picture in front of me. I knew one other guy that was on the team from Austin: Elmus Peterson, a big kid who played at Travis High School. Peterson was a good football player. I had to get him out of jail the day before we left for school. I don't even remember what he did. I just knew that I was going to borrow whatever it took from Dad to bail out Peterson. No way was I going to Ranger alone.

**Ranger, Texas, was just like the West Texas you see in the movies. There were tumbleweeds everywhere. There was no locker room. The football team was expected to dress in the dorms and come to practice in uniform. Ranger was a town where they might have sent convicts to live for some heinous crime.**

I was the only one with a truck. Every time I wanted to go somewhere, I had 30 guys jumping in the back of my truck. I unloaded my stuff into the dorm. My dorm room was the smallest room I had ever seen, much less lived in. I watched my mom and dad drive away and then it hit me. I was alone in Ranger, Texas. I had a terrific roommate, the team's long snapper. Good guy, but that didn't relieve my homesick feelings. I had a girlfriend in Austin that I liked. I had never been away from home to speak of. My dad told my mom, "If that boy stays more than two days, then he is tougher than I am." I lasted four.

Football was a shambles. I didn't know three guys on the team. I loved high school football because everyone knew each other and we fought like hell for each other. At Ranger, nobody gave a shit about anyone. Of course, four days might have been a bit hasty to toss a net over the entire program. I didn't care. I had a case of homesickness like you wouldn't believe. I called my dad and told him one thing before he could say a word.

"Dad, whatever you do, do not tell me that I can't come home."

Dad said, "If you come home, then you'll never play football again. If you can deal with that, then I guess that I'll see you soon."

That was enough for me. I started loading my truck immediately. I had 10 guys helping me within five minutes, and every one of them wanted to go with me. I told them all to stop thinking about leaving. Shit, my family had a ranch and I had a job to go back to. I didn't need football, and I sure as hell didn't need football in a place like Ranger, Texas. I tried to call coach Hatch. No answer. I gave my roommate my icebox so I wouldn't have to load it into my truck again. I said good-bye to a couple of guys and I drove like Dale Earnhardt back to Austin. Coach Hatch called me the next morning. When he called, he tried to convince me to return. I explained that it was time for me to work with my family and be a cowboy.

The day after I returned from Ranger, I went into Austin and moved in with my friend Cuatro. Cuatro Hollen and I had grown up together. I showed up at Cuatro's apartment in the Northwest Hills section of Austin and told him that I was moving in. He had no objections. When it hit me that I was that attached to my family, it scared me a little. I knew then that I had to become my own man. I didn't have to do it in Ranger, but I couldn't do it living at home my whole life.

So Cuatro and I lived the college lifestyle without the school. I worked at the saddle shop, and we partied

OK, so maybe I wasn't the greatest student in the world, but I made it through high school. And I was done with college in just four days!

in Austin every night. We went to the bars and got into some kind of trouble every weekend. On Wednesdays, we would go to the Post Oak Ranch, Thursdays were spent at Dance Across Texas, and the weekends were spent on Sixth Street in Austin. We didn't start any trouble, but we certainly had the mentality to finish anything that might have slid

**I explained that it was time for me to work with my family and be a cowboy.**

our way. We wanted it that way. We spent more than a few nights posting bail. Cuatro and I had a pact involving jail: if one went without the other, then the one in jail would use his only phone call to call the other. I had to tell Cuatro how much I missed him if I got thrown in jail without him. The amazing aspect of those days was the fact that we did not slow down after getting banned from more than a few clubs.

At the Post Oak Ranch, they employed a security staff to work the club and patrol the parking lots. The parking lots were large. After an evening cut short by another fight, Cuatro and I were escorted to the main exit. While we were receiving a lecture from the police and security personnel outside the front door, Cuatro and I looked at each other and we had the same thought. Instead of listening to the speech that surrounded our impending fall from grace, Cuatro and I jumped into the security golf cart and drove down a long flight of stairs. The cops and security guards chased us on foot. Thank goodness that golf cart was unusually fast and the cops and security guards had spent a little too much time at Dunkin' Donuts.

On many nights, we wound up on the University of Texas campus. After going to a frat party one night at UT, Cuatro and I managed to drink way too much of their trash-can punch. Trash-can punch was a mixture of any and all hard liquors and a splash of Kool-Aid. The mixture was normally served in a full-sized trashcan. I have heard recently that the frat boys piss in the punch. Make a note, if you are ever at a frat party and the frat boys are not drinking the punch, then I highly recommend B.Y.O.B.

Anyway, Cuatro and I put away plenty of trash-can punch and couldn't manage to find any trouble. Frat boys can be well-behaved when two drunken cowboys crash their house. We left in Cuatro's shit-heap, which originally was a Ford-F150, year unknown. After we stopped for gas, I stepped out of the truck to use the payphone. I called a girl I knew to get together. I must not have liked what she said, but I had so much trash-can punch in me that I barely remember making the call. I walked over to the truck and added a new dent with my fist to the front quarter panel of Cuatro's truck. Hell, there were so many dents it was hard to notice. Cuatro didn't see it that way. He got mad as hell. I apologized, but the apology wasn't enough. Cuatro was fuming. I told him to get over it. I had apologized and it was time to move on. Cuatro told me to step outside and we would figure the whole thing out and handle it like a couple of drunk men! I was getting the best of my friend when the cops arrived. The cops wanted to know what was going on, but all Cuatro could say was that he was pressing charges against me. He swears to this day that he said he wasn't pressing charges, but we both know better. We both got hauled to jail.

Living with Cuatro was a special time in my life. I may not rank it as the most productive time in my life, but those days were unforgettable. Cuatro and I are still great friends today. We had college without the homework or pressure of grades. Life was beautiful. I missed football, but hindsight is worthless.

I should have walked on at Southwest Texas University. They didn't show enough interest in me to offer a scholarship, so coach Dowdy referred me to the one school that appeared to offer a full ride. As I said before, it turned out the scholarship wasn't a full ride, and the other schools interested in me backed away because of my size or my scholastic record. My scholastic record consisted of the easiest courses available. I could have made the team at Southwest and I would have been close to home. I could have enrolled on academic probation, but I wanted the scholarship. It sounded better. Coach Dowdy went to a small school for two years then went on to play at Texas and became an All-American. I saw myself doing that. I thought I could play at Ranger for two years and then move up to a Division I school. SWTU is only 45 minutes from Austin. I have wondered many times about how far I could have gone had I continued to play football or made some other choice about school and football. But hell, Cuatro was the one who talked me into team roping, which led to bulldogging.

I never wanted to be decent at sports. I wanted to be the best. I wanted to be the wild guy that made a statement. I wanted to be the next Brian Bosworth. Since I can remember, the Boz had always been my hero. Not only was he the toughest and the best linebacker, he was wild and in your face. To this day, I will still defend that guy. He was the best. When I quit football, I knew that void had to be filled or I would go nuts. It didn't take long.

# 7

# The NFR, Round Three, 2002

Two nights down, and eight more rounds to go. I had placed in each of the first two rounds. The Finals were all about survival. I had to stay in the average hunt and hope to win a couple of go-rounds. The steers dictated which go-rounds were winnable and which go-rounds you simply wanted to make a decent run and possibly place. I was approaching the third round, and I still didn't know the steers in the draw. After the third round, the steers were not new anymore. If I got by the third round without any damage, then the playing field was level.

I was thinking that my horse, Boss, had worked well, and I was going to stay on him throughout the Finals. Boss was comfortable to ride, and I really believe that a blind man could have ridden him. He backed himself into the box and waited. I had to cowboy, or maneuver, the hell out of Slim Shady. Shady was a mental case, but faster than a bottle rocket. When I was on Shady, I had to be thinking all the time. I had to work my feet to get him situated and my hands to keep his head straight. At the Finals I was willing to give up some speed to ride an easier horse. Too many things could happen on Shady. Boss was a comfortable shoe, and I thought I needed that fit to continue after the first two rounds.

In case you couldn't tell, I was pretty pumped up after the third round: in the money three times in a row. (Photo courtesy of Mike Copeman Photography)

My best friends were rolling in and out of town, and they all gave me tremendous support. Las Vegas has a plethora of shit to distract anyone who is there to be distracted. Some guys in the NFR are afraid to go out because of the distractions. The general consensus was to avoid the bars and casinos if you were competing. Most guys would grab an early dinner and try to get some sleep. I fell in the middle. I get bored in casinos after 15 minutes. For the most part, casinos are full of a collection of schmucks in bad clothes who are convinced they can break the bank once they find a streak. Let me tell you, they didn't build the casinos because they lose money. Giving money away for no reason is not a recreational activity that I crave. I made a point to go out and spend some time with the people that mean the most to me. Between my family and friends, my down time was not spent wallowing in my room about the next round. Their support was more important to me than they will ever know.

> For the most part, casinos are full of a collection of schmucks in bad clothes who are convinced they can break the bank once they find a streak.

The third round was upon us. I caught a decent steer in the third round and threw him down in four seconds flat. I thought Boss worked decently and I placed fourth, another money round. Joey Bell won the third go. Cash Myers came in sixth and Bill Pace took second. These were the guys that would be there at the end. I felt good about my round. I felt good about Boss, and I was convinced more than ever that I could win a world championship on Boss.

# 8

# Rodeo, Bulldogging, and a Commitment

It didn't take me long to understand that my future was not working at the saddle shop and fighting my way into the realms of lore on Sixth Street. Cattle ranching was too much work. A few of my escapades had landed me on thin ice and probation with the Austin Police Department.

Cuatro suggested that we start team roping. A friend who worked at the saddle shop, Mike Slover, talked to me about it on many occasions. Mike is a team roper and continues to manage the saddle shop to this day. Considering how full my plate was at the time, team roping seemed like something less likely to land me in jail than my barroom antics.

I talked to my dad about team roping, and he agreed to purchase a horse and trailer if I would stay out of trouble.

Cuatro and I began practicing at Dennis Scott's ranch. Man, do I feel sorry for those two horses that Cuatro and I rode to begin our rodeo careers. We roped for three hours when we practiced and then loaded the horses in the trailer and drove down to the local tavern to get hammered. The horses sat outside in the trailer while we got shit-faced. Then someone told us about watering the horses.

Team roping is a two-man event. I took the header position and became fairly good at it in a short period of time. Cuatro and I would go to some local team ropings, and the best we could do was win a buckle and a few bucks—which, at the time, was fine with us. The best thing about the whole experience for me was to be competitive again. I started to take team roping seriously, and the competition became an adrenaline high.

I remember talking to Dad about roping. He said that with my aggressive nature, maybe I should try tackling steers instead of roping them. My mom called Joe Morris, a close friend of the family. Morris was past 40 years old when I began to work with him, and he still competes today, past the age of 50. Mom asked him to help me get started in steer wrestling. He has lived his entire life in Elgin, Texas, about 16 miles north of Bastrop. He has been bulldogging since he was 17. Morris never questioned my intentions or assessed the possibilities of my success. Here I was, 19 years old and a few ticks shy of 200 pounds. I had never thrown a steer, and my riding ability was basic at best. Morris told me that no one was too small to bulldog, and there were no experience requirements that he was aware of. If you entered and won, they didn't ask you how long you had been doing it.

Morris started me on sliding dummies attached to a tractor. The purpose of this exercise was to work on my footwork. My hours water-skiing, barefoot-water-skiing, and wake-boarding paid off. I graduated in one day to throwing down some steers from the ground. I stood next to the chute and caught the steers as they were released. Morris' wife, Sue, taped the entire practice. I remember

My first rodeo experiences were in calf roping, before my dad wisely suggested that with my aggressive nature, I might make a pretty good steer wrestler.

taking the tape of the first day throwing steers and showing it to a girl that I was dating. She was pretty impressed and that nailed it for me. I had found a sport that was much more physical than team roping, for which I felt I had a natural talent, and which girls dug.

Morris and I worked hard together that fall of 1994. I got my Professional Rodeo Cowboys Association permit in early 1995. Morris never lost his patience with me during those practice days. I cannot say the same thing about myself. I wanted to be good from day one, and it didn't work that way. I was the one screaming at myself when I messed up. Morris could have gotten on me harder, but I did a good enough job of that on my own. I never questioned Morris' advice. Joe Morris had a full-time job and went to rodeos on weekends or whenever he could. I respected Joe for the work ethic he demonstrated by working first and bulldogging when he could. He epitomized the ideal of responsibility for family and home. Rodeo cowboys are infamous for sacrificing everything to chase an elusive buckle that most never come close to winning. Morris could have chucked everything and traveled off to pursue his dream, but life wasn't just about him. So many guys never understand that.

Morris took me to my first rodeo as a steer wrestler in Victoria, Texas. I saw guys that I had been reading about. I just didn't want to fall off my horse the wrong way or take a face plant in the arena floor. Morris often kidded me about my horsemanship, or the lack of it. He always told me that I had the ability to ride a horse far enough to catch a steer, but any further was a stretch. Saying I was nervous while waiting in the box for that first run is an understatement. I caught my steer at my first professional rodeo. I had to wrestle around with the steer some, but I was happy as hell that I even caught him.

> **Rodeo cowboys are infamous for sacrificing everything to chase an elusive buckle that most never come close to winning.**

In the spring of 1995, when the PRCA rodeo in Austin came around, I saw Todd Fox in the parking lot near the arena. Todd Fox is a steer wrestling legend. I approached him and told him that I was throwing steers and I wanted to learn from the best. I asked him if he would help me. He looked at me and asked if I had ever been to the weekly rodeo in Mesquite, Texas. I told him no. He told me to get ready because Friday night we were heading that way.

When we got to the Mesquite rodeo, I couldn't believe that I was traveling with Todd Fox. I wanted to do well, but I wanted to do well for Fox. I didn't want him thinking he was wasting his time with me. That night I broke the barrier. (The barrier is a line stretched across the contestant's box. If the horse crosses the barrier before the steer has cleared his rope, the cowboy receives a 10-second penalty.) My time would have been 3.9 seconds. I was that close; 3.9 seconds would have won Mesquite that week. Driving home that night, Fox's driver, Slick, was up front guiding the one-ton diesel truck and horse trailer. Fox and I were in the back of the rig, stretched out in the camper. Fox was snoring loudly enough to blend with the even hum of the diesel engine. I laid there and watched the night sky as it soared high above Texas. I

> **I caught my steer at my first professional rodeo. I had to wrestle around with the steer some, but I was happy as hell that I even caught him.**

knew then what I wanted. I had been to rodeos sporadically, every two weeks or so. How cool was this life? I noticed a bunch of guys in Mesquite running to catch their rigs as soon as the rodeo was over. Trucks and rigs were wasting no time in moving out. I asked Fox what the big rush was. He told me that those guys were going to Scottsdale, Arizona, then to El Paso, and then back to San Antonio. It was a big weekend, and those guys might make it to three separate rodeos over the next two days.

I thought that would be great. There was more than one rodeo every two weeks. That was what I wanted to do.

Fox and I started traveling together whenever his schedule allowed. We went to some Texas spring rodeos. The first rodeo that I placed in was at Huntsville, Texas, in 1995. It was raining in Huntsville and my run took place in the mud. After I won that first check, I was pissed if I didn't place every time.

Fox was just what the doctor had ordered for me. Joe Morris was good for me when I started, but very even tempered. I needed to be pushed harder. Fox was a ball of testosterone. He got me pumped up for every rodeo.

"Let's go win some money tonight!" Fox would yell at me when we arrived at our destination. "Let's check out our steers and get ready to kick some ass, boy!"

I loved that enthusiasm. I fed on it. I bought my first horse from him. He basically gave me the horse. He had used Bailey for a long time and was getting ready to work in a new horse. He sold Bailey to me for less than $5,000. In rodeo, you can't buy a half-lame horse for $5,000. Fox gave me his saddle and practically put me in business that year. He also gave me his trailer and all the tack that I needed. He even let me use his hazing horse. Todd Fox was considered by many to be the best steer wrestler in the world. He had made me his project, and I could not have been happier. Fox made the NFR from 1986–1995. He went into the Finals ranked number one in the world on more than one occasion. Everyone had their own opinion on why Fox never

Me and my first rodeo horse, Bailey, which I bought from my good buddy Todd Fox in 1995.

won the world championship, but no one could ever say that there was a better steer wrestler for those 10 years. I've always said that to win a title you have to have the stars lined up right and the talent to pull it off. I guess those stars never lined up right for him to become the world champion, but everyone knew he had the talent. I have often wondered if my championship buckle was for both of us.

Fox was going to quit in 1995. He didn't have a good run to start the year. I think the only reason that he went was because I bugged him to death about traveling with me. I would get to Marble Falls to pick him up for a rodeo, and he would walk out and tell me to go ahead without him. He would say, "Take the horses and you go on without me."

I remember telling him, "Man, you have to come with me. I don't want to go alone. I need you, man."

I think he finally relented each week because I was so pathetic. Shit, I think I sounded like a little kid afraid to go to school without his older brother. The truth was not that far away from the irony of a self-proclaimed bad-ass steer wrestler begging his mentor not to abandon him. Fox eventually credited me for him making the NFR in 1995. He invited me to Las Vegas to spend the entire week with him. I decided to go to Vegas on my 21$^{st}$ birthday, December 8. It was the eighth round, and I couldn't wait to see Fox. That night he tore his knee up, which ended his career. I remember his dad taking me down the elevator to see him in the sports medicine room. As soon as Fox saw me, he began to cry. So did I. I wanted him to win the championship so badly that year. I knew at that point it wouldn't happen, and I had also lost my traveling partner. I loved traveling with Fox. It was like a tie-down roper traveling with Roy Cooper, Fred Whitfield, or Joe Beaver. He has since gone on to become very successful in his family's real estate business. Maybe one day he'll have to show me how to do that too.

Fox's reputation kept him pretty clean by the time we traveled together. Rodeo was about respect earned inside the arena and respect earned outside the arena. Determination and talent earned one kind. A hard head and an iron fist earned the other. By the start of the season in 1995, no one in his right mind wanted to mess with Todd Fox. He would freely admit to more than his fair share of bad choices in his younger days. Todd Fox was one tough guy. Bar fights used to find their way to him, but they rarely continued once he stepped in. He always spoke his mind. It didn't much matter to him if he hurt your feelings or offended you; Fox was brutally honest. I respected him for more than just that, but he had balls. Even when he knew the odds were against him, he continued to speak his mind. I always admired that. He loved being a cowboy. He always told me that the cowboy life was the coolest life we would ever lead, and we wouldn't know that until we gave it up.

Because Fox couldn't rodeo anymore, I looked for someone to take with me. Cuatro came along to many Texas rodeos. We had gone to a rodeo in Athens, Texas, later that year, a good four-hour drive from Austin. The slack didn't end until nearly 2:00 in the morning. I drove after we loaded up and started for home. After less than 30 minutes, I turned to Cuatro and announced that I wasn't even tired. Cuatro concurred and announced that he wasn't tired either. I slammed on the brakes, pulled over, and said, "Good! You drive." I hopped in the back seat of the truck and went to sleep. Cuatro took over the wheel and swore he would never go to one of my rodeos again.

Later that year I placed in both rounds in Yoakum, Texas, and won the average. The total take from that rodeo filled my permit, and I was a full member of the Professional Rodeo Cowboys Association. I called Mom and Dad. When good things happened to me, I called my folks. When bad things happened to me, I called my folks. I liked calling them, and I sure as hell never apologized to anyone for calling my mom and dad.

> **Rodeo was about respect earned inside the arena and respect earned outside the arena. Determination and talent earned one kind. A hard head and an iron fist earned the other.**

After my success at Yoakum, my mom told me to enter Greeley, Colorado. That was one of the biggest rodeos of the summer. Whoa! I didn't know if I was ready to take that step yet. Greeley was a lot bigger rodeo than I had ever been to, and I looked for every excuse not to go. I told Mom my PRCA card would take a few weeks to be approved. She didn't buy that. Leave it to Mom to throw me to the wolves.

Mom got my paperwork in order with the PRCA, and I hopped a plane to Greeley, the biggest Fourth of July rodeo in the country. I had no idea what horse I'd be riding or who was going to haze for me. All I knew was that I was entered in Greeley on July 4, 1995. Mom and Dad knew a bareback rider from Greeley named Bob Logue. Logue picked me up at the airport and I stayed at his house.

I made it out to the arena and found Alfalfa Fedderson. I had ridden Fedderson's horse a few times before because he hazed for Fox. I asked him if I could ride his horse. He agreed and we went to check out the steer that I had drawn.

It was raining like a flood. All the past records on my steer were no times. No one had ever caught him. All of these experienced steer wrestlers had no time on the steer I had drawn. I read that Roy Duvall missed the same steer earlier in the year. Roy Duvall had been to the NFR 24 times and had won three world championship titles. Everyone called him the Legend, if that tells you anything. Duvall is a big man and maybe one of the toughest men ever to rodeo. He knew my dad well, so I didn't feel completely lost walking up to him. I asked him about the steer. All he said was that I shouldn't worry about that steer. "That steer stops," Duvall told me. "Son, it's just what you call a bad draw. You can't catch him."

Well, I did catch him. I was 3.9 seconds on that steer. It felt like an out-of-body experience. I woke up and I had dropped the steer. That was the biggest rodeo in the country that week, and I was winning the go-round. I was competing against legends and NFR finalists. I wound up winning $1,400 that trip and thought that there would never be another poor day on tour. I had doubled my earnings in one day. I was 20 years old and had been a bulldogger for eight months.

The first buckle I won was in Vinita, Oklahoma. After my run, I heard these two old guys talking. One of them turned to me and told me they should just give me the buckle right now because they wouldn't beat my time. My eyes lit up. "Buckle?" I asked, "This rodeo

**"Son, it's just what you call a bad draw. You can't catch him."**

gives out buckles?" Not all of the smaller rodeos handed out buckles for winning. Wow, I thought, if I could win a buckle, I would have one of my own and wouldn't have to wear Dad's anymore. I had always been proud to wear my dad's buckles, but I felt a little odd wearing a bull-riding buckle. When my buckle arrived in the mail a couple of weeks later, it was pretty cool, but there were no stones. I took the buckle to my jeweler and had two rubies put into the flowers on the buckle. My mom told me to cool it with the stones because I would win plenty more buckles. I thought, yeah, right! That buckle could have been my only buckle and I was going to deck it out.

The year 1995 was a learning experience for me. We went to rodeos across the West at the end of the summer. I also went to Cheyenne for the first time. I wound up going to the Cow Palace in San Francisco at the end of the year.

Todd Fox said it would be good for me, but I think he said that just so he didn't have to go alone. He thought that the experience of going to the Cow Palace would be good practice for the future. The Cow Palace was the last rodeo of the year prior to the Finals. If I would need a good finish at the Cow Palace in future years to lock down a spot at the NFR, then the experience in 1995 would prove invaluable.

At the end of 1995, I asked Fox if I had the fundamentals to be better than average. I didn't want to be an average bulldogger; I wanted to be the best. Todd told me that I could accomplish everything I wanted to do in rodeo if I conquered the mental barriers. He told me that I had the grit and the ability to succeed and be a world-class bulldogger. What he told me that day and eventually taught me over the next three years got me to where I wanted to go.

Fox instilled in me the notion that I could not find any shortcuts to a title. Hell, I tried like hell to find one, but there were none to be found. I stormed out of practice sessions with him. I stormed out of rodeo arenas after I fell on my face. I announced many times, "I quit!" I would say that I didn't need the bullshit of traveling and I was headed home. The one thing Fox taught me more than anything else when I made such proclamations was that nobody cared. Nobody cared if Sid Steiner went home or quit practicing. It wasn't until I realized that no one did care if I quit that I became a force to be reckoned with. It took Todd Fox to teach me that good starts and flat falls were the only things that won rodeos.

After 1995 my mind was made up to pursue rodeo. My mom and dad had both made the NFR, and that's what I wanted to do. I remember telling people on more than one occasion that I was double-bred NFR, and there would be no way to keep me out. Dad had an arena built on the ranch and brought in a couple of dozen steers. We had lights put up and the dirt brought in to make a good foundation. I knew that the more steers I could get my hands on, the better I would become. Each month was a huge step. During the winter

**I announced many times, "I quit!" I would say that I didn't need the bullshit of traveling and I was headed home. It wasn't until I realized that no one did care if I quit that I became a force to be reckoned with.**

of 1996, I practiced hard. I was not an easy person to practice with. Fox's work with me had not been completed, and I was still an ass in the practice pen. I wanted to run more steers than anyone else in the event. Since I could remember, I liked to practice. This was true in baseball, and it was scary how true it was in football. I liked to work out at the gym when I wasn't running steers because it made me a better bulldogger. Don't get me wrong: I like to look good too, but those days in the gym

**My mom and dad had both made the NFR, and that's what I wanted to do. I remember telling people on more than one occasion that I was double-bred NFR, and there would be no way to keep me out.**

were kicked to a much higher level because I wanted to be the best at my sport. My dad asked me how I thought I was going to beat all of those guys that grew up riding horses and rodeoing from the time they learned to walk. I told Dad that I would outwork them. I could throw 30 or 40 steers per day when they were throwing maybe 8 or 10 at best. They might practice twice a week, but I would

practice every day. If I wasn't throwing steers down, I was at the gym lifting weights.

I kicked everything when the runs didn't go well. I kicked the chutes. I kicked at the steers if they got by me. I cussed the steers. If People for the Ethical Treatment of Animals (PETA) had a camera on me during those practice days, they would have locked me up and thrown away the key. I threw punches at some steers. I even threw dirt in their eyes. I never set out to hurt the steers, though. I have only hurt two steers in my career. One steer broke his leg during my run at a rodeo up north, and the other broke his neck in a freak run in Wichita Falls, Texas. Both times I cried. Hell, I don't hunt and never understood the recreation in killing animals. Based on my practice antics, that would have been a hard sell, though.

My attitude was bad, and I was still throwing fits. I remember traveling with Rusty Sewalt to a rodeo in Ellensburg, Washington. Sewalt was a calf roper that everyone called Flipper. He won the first round in calf roping, and I won the first round of the bulldogging. Flipper and I went out after the rodeo and celebrated. We drank margaritas and were on cloud nine. The next day was the start of the second go. He missed his calf, and I missed my steer. I was supposed to be on the road for another month, but I was mad and I wanted to go home. I walked out to the rig to see him throwing his bags out of the trailer. I asked Flipper, a three-time NFR qualifier, what was going on.

"I'm catching a plane home. Do you wanna go?" Rusty asked.

"Hell yes," I replied.

Rusty didn't have to ask me twice. We were headed to the airport before the dust settled. That's the way rodeo was for me. You had to learn to handle the highs and the lows. I never really mastered that.

My dad and everyone else that had ever practiced with me went through the same stuff. They all walked out of practice on many occasions, telling me that they would never practice with me again. Eddie Joseph, a close friend of mine, stuck it out through most of my tantrums and ran steers with me when no one else would. He was a big reason why I never quit. I cried on the arena floor after practice many times. It meant that much to me. It was personal to me. At night, I would watch tapes from past NFR performances and search for reasons why one run was better than the next. I pictured myself at my first NFR and I formed mental pictures of winning a title. I was determined to work harder than anybody else and I think I did. I wanted to hurry up and be great.

I went out on the road in 1996 with Frank Davis and Dale Meinecke. Going into 1996, I thought I was better than I really was. I remember telling Byron Walker, 16-time NFR qualifier and two-time world champ, that I was better than he was. He later proved me wrong when he beat me in a match we had in 2000. Dodge City, Kansas, and Tucson, Arizona, were big wins for me. At the end of 1996, I hooked up with Butch Stokes. Stokes was 46 years old and had competed at different levels of rodeo, but never made the NFR as a competitor. Stokes' family never had enough money to buy a decent bulldogging horse, so he taught himself how to train his own horses. Over the years, he became one of the most respected names when it came to bulldogging horses. Stokes traveled with and provided the horses for the best steer wrestlers over the past 20 years. He traveled with Steve Duhon, Butch Myers, Tommy Puryear, Tom Ferguson, Stan Williamson, and Roy Duvall. He was like a swing coach for the best. Stokes used to talk to me about learning how to

> **I was determined to work harder than anybody else and I think I did. I wanted to hurry up and be great.**

lose and how to handle losing. He believed in the natural progression of becoming the best. Todd Fox never wanted to hear a thing about losing. Fox told me to start winning, then I wouldn't have to worry about how to handle losing.

Stokes and I talked about horses for hours. I wasn't much of an accomplished rider, and Butch was the first one to really talk to me about the dynamics of riding in our event. I didn't know how to manage a horse in the box. Nobody had given me the structure of the box before. Where should I set the horse's nose? How do I set the tension in my hands? How do I set the tie-down? Butch told me that I didn't need to be an accomplished horseman, but I needed to understand what it took to ride a world-class bulldogging horse. Hand placement is critical. The time difference between the steer's release and the horse's release is so small, that the smallest mistake is catastrophic for the run.

**Stokes used to talk to me about learning how to lose and how to handle losing. He believed in the natural progression of becoming the best. Todd Fox never wanted to hear a thing about losing. Fox told me to start winning, then I wouldn't have to worry about how to handle losing.**

We drove everywhere looking for the right horse. Stokes told me that I had to find a great horse to take me to another level. We finally found a little horse owned by Wade Lewis. The horse was for sale, but not cheap. Teece had left me some money for college, and because I wasn't going to college and had no plans to return anytime in the next 200 years, I took the money and bought a horse, a hazing horse, and a trailer.

Once a competitor begins a full-time rodeo career, the complications begin to set in. Aside from the work ethic and the high level of competition at every rodeo, entering rodeos becomes a full-time job. In 2000, the first year that I made the Finals, I competed in 98 rodeos. In 2002 I competed in 72 rodeos, and I went home two months before the season ended. Organizing your own schedule can be one of the most complicated aspects of competing. The whole process is orchestrated by ProCom, the computer central entry system that filled each rodeo event slot.

Rodeo travel has always been a brutal constant within the sport, especially for those of us toting horses along. We left for Denver at the beginning of 1997. Stokes and I had a lot of good times at rodeos during that year. The best thing that he did was to keep my head on straight. I continued to act like an asshole when I didn't do well. I kicked everything in sight and swore so bad that I embarrassed myself. Stokes kept a lid on my head. He was great at working my anger into a positive energy flow: "Oh, Sid, you are so competitive." You know, blah, blah, blah, but it worked. By the time I got to the next rodeo, I was fired up and ready to rock. Every time someone asked him if I was any good, he replied, "Tiger Woods. This kid is the next Tiger Woods!" He had me believing it.

The only time Stokes lost his temper with me was in early 1997. I was having a rough time on the road and wasn't winning. I kept questioning him about my horse running wide. The horse was preventing me from catching the steers where I wanted to catch them or causing me to miss them completely. After numerous pleas to get Stokes to agree with my assessment on the failures of my horse, he finally turned and looked at me with a look I had never seen before.

"Sid," Stokes began, sounding fatherly, "you are riding like a sack of shit. The horse has nothing to do with it!"

He grimaced and turned back to driving the truck. He looked a little nervous about telling me that I rode like a sack of shit. After a moment of silence, I busted out laughing. Stokes busted out laughing and I think we almost ran that truck off the road we were laughing so hard. I always appreciated it when someone told me the truth.

In 1997 I finished 18th in the world. To say that I had taken a big step from starting just three years prior to finishing among the top 20 in the world was an understatement in the grandest scale.

I met Jamie in the fall of 1998. I was going through a rough time in my career, but she made me want to get better—and I did.

I worked hard during the entire 1997 rodeo season. At the start of 1998, I didn't win much during the winter and I had reached a point where I wanted to quit. I just didn't have it in me anymore. So, I went home. Byron Walker called me at home. He told me that I had too much talent to quit and to get my butt up to his place and bring my horse.

I found renewed inspiration when I lost Teece—my best friend—in the fall of 1999.

I went out with Walker for the second half of 1998. I started to win again, but got cold just as fast. In the fall of 1998, I met Jamie Richards, my future wife. I was at a bad part of my career when we met. I was frustrated and sick of not winning. There was something about Jamie that made me want to be better. I didn't want Jamie's boyfriend to be the guy that sucked, so I began to practice even harder. Jamie and I worked well together. I had a shot to make the Finals in 1999. It would have been a long shot, but it was possible.

Then my mom's dad, who I called Papa, passed away around the Fourth of July that year. I took a chartered plane to Oklahoma for the funeral. My grandmother delayed the funeral for two days so I could make it. That took something out of me emotionally. Later that fall, Teece died and that nearly killed me. Teece was my best friend. He was one of the main reasons I got into rodeo. It still bothers me that Teece never got to see me win a world championship. When he died, I just hit the ground and said screw it. Dad flew me home from Albuquerque, New Mexico. A bunch of my rodeo traveling partners and competitors showed up and gave me all the support they could. They all wanted to know if I was coming back that year.

I didn't.

# 9

# The NFR, Round Four, 2002

Night four was my birthday. I had placed in all three rounds and now we knew the steers. My plan was on course as we approached the fourth day of the Finals. When I went to walk Boss, however, as I usually did each day, my heart sank. He couldn't put any weight on his front foot. I was pissed off. I am not one to change when things are working. Boss had worked well during the first three rounds. He was leaving off my hand on cue and I was catching my steers where I wanted to catch them. I had placed in all three rounds and the last thing I wanted to do was switch horses.

I felt myself slipping back to the negative thought process. Jamie reminded me how good Shady had worked

Despite having to switch horses for the fourth round, I placed again and stayed on target. (Photo courtesy of Mike Copeman Photography)

all year. To me, Shady was a gamble, but then again, this was Vegas. My fourth round steer was a runner. I was concerned that it was going to take me too long to catch the steer. I was first out in the fourth round and I hated going first. Shady jammed. He took off from my hand and ran that steer down with ease. I was 4.2 seconds, and I placed in the fourth round.

I had a plan and it was working. I wanted to stay in the average hunt and keep placing. If I had a steer that I could win the go-round on, then I would, but I was determined not to do anything stupid. I thought about the two things that Todd Fox always wished for me: good starts and flat falls.

**If I had a steer that I could win the go-round on, then I would, but I was determined not to do anything stupid.**

As each round progressed, I gained confidence. I wanted to have each and every person who helped me get to the Finals around me. That was more important to me than it was to them. The more people that I had in my corner for the Finals, the more confident I became.

# 10

# Jamie

It was obvious to me that because my parents had married young they had a chance to get closer to their kids than parents that chose to marry at a later age had. My parents were always able to relate to the problems that Shane and I went through. I always wanted that for myself. I had never put a date on when I would get married, but I knew that I wanted kids.

Jamie Richards was traveling with Danyelle Campbell, who was a friend of mine. I had never heard of Jamie Richards and she had never heard of Sid Steiner. The first time we met was under typical circumstances for me. I was coming out of a bar in Caldwell, Idaho. The bar was right next to the rodeo grounds. After a few rounds of beer with my friends, I got into a small skirmish on my way to the bathroom. While my new friend was catching up with the planks on the barroom floor, I was scurrying out the front door because the police had been summoned. As I was crossing the parking lot, Campbell's truck pulled in with a few girls. Of course I had time to stop and chat, but time was limited. Jamie Richards had just met her future husband. I can't imagine a better way to impress a girl than to excuse yourself while in the middle of a conversation and then to break out in a dead run when a police car pulls up. Maybe she should have realized what she was getting into right then.

The next day, I came out to the arena to exercise my horse. Jamie and Campbell were saddling their horses. They asked me if I would help them set up the barrels. I knew that I wanted to get to know Jamie from the first time we met. Jamie was small, cute, blonde, and had a great personality.

Jamie was from Kennewick, Washington. Kennewick was about three hours southeast of Seattle. Jamie's family lived on 25 acres and always had horses around. Her first experience on a horse came when she was one month old. She got a pony when she was six, and her first horse came not long after the pony. Jerry and Suzanne Richards raised their daughter to show horses and run barrels. Jamie started to take barrel racing seriously when she was a sophomore in high school. She has had her Women's Professional Rodeo Association card since 1996. A friend convinced Jamie to travel with her and they both set out on the pro circuit. Jamie was ranked ninth in the world when we met.

Jamie's family did not have much money, which to me made Jamie that much more attractive. She reminded me of my mom. I looked at that as the ultimate compliment.

Jamie was making the most out of limited resources. My mom came from a similar background in Fort Supply, Oklahoma. Dad saw the same things in my mom that I saw in Jamie. Someone asked me once if I was trying to be my dad. I didn't have to think about that question long. The answer was yes. There was no one that I had ever met that was

> **I can't imagine a better way to impress a girl than to excuse yourself while in the middle of a conversation and then to break out in a dead run when a police car pulls up.**

like my dad. I have admired many people and they have meant the world to me, but no one comes close to my dad. If I turn out like him, then great! That would be just fine with me. People have always told me that I did this or that just like my dad. I see nothing wrong with that comparison.

When we had a chance to talk, Jamie was surprised to find out that I called my mom and dad at least three times each day. Meeting a guy who reinforced the rodeo cowboy stereotype and who also got homesick and missed his parents threw her for a loop. After Caldwell, I couldn't wait to get to another rodeo so I could talk to Jamie. I come from a really strong family. Jamie comes from a great family. Jamie's dad was a jockey and then became a trainer, so he was gone all the time. Jamie's mom was very supportive of Jamie and her riding and went to all her shows and competitions. I have always gotten along well with both of Jamie's parents.

> **Someone asked me once if I was trying to be my dad. I didn't have to think about that question long. The answer was yes. There was no one that I had ever met that was like my dad.**

In the fall of 1998 Teece and I flew to Albuquerque, New Mexico, to meet Jamie. My granddad had some horses running in New Mexico, and I had been talking about Jamie since I met her.

We met again in Oklahoma City, Oklahoma. Jamie had all but made the Finals in 1998 when her horse needed a break and quit running. When we left Oklahoma City, Jamie didn't know what to do, so I suggested that she load up the horse in my trailer and come back to Austin with me. We were six hours away from Austin, where we could go see the best vets in the country. Dr. Lewis and Dr. Hayes practiced 10 miles from the ranch in Bastrop. I told Jamie that we would get her horse running again. The vets said the horse was run down and we turned her out at the ranch. Jamie was a little intimidated about coming to Bastrop. The horses were loaded up and Jamie was about to get her first taste of the Steiner family in Texas.

At the ranch, we ran into a group of cowboys and my dad. It was late afternoon and they had the back end of a truck opened to a cooler of beer. I introduced Jamie and we headed to the house. Jamie didn't realize that the long-haired guy sitting on the back of the truck was my dad. We went to Sixth Street in Austin every night and partied with my friends.

At the end of the year, Jamie had to go to the Cow Palace in San Francisco for the last rodeo of the year. This was her last shot to make the Finals in 1998. Jamie got a

Jamie and me at the Rodeo Hall of Fame.

new truck in Austin. We loaded her horse and drove to New Mexico. I flew back to Austin from there and Jamie drove alone to San Francisco. Jamie and I had talked about the Finals. She assumed that I would be there to support her. I told her that I would never go to the Finals if I didn't make it as a competitor. That was me. I was that competitive. People can always read and assess their own faults, but reading and changing are two separate issues. I didn't want to change. My competitive nature was going to take me places someday and I had no desire to tone that down. After the short round in San Francisco, Jamie called me crying. She had finished 16th and missed making the NFR by less than $200. I asked her to come back to Texas, and she never left. We traveled and lived together from the start of 1999.

Mom asked me what I was going to get Jamie for Christmas. I told Mom that I had this really nice bracelet picked out for Jamie. Mom looked at me and I knew what she was thinking. She told me that I had better not let this one slip away. Dad was there and he told me pretty much the same thing. My family loved this girl and I loved her too. The Steiners are a close-knit group, and when we get together, there are only a few people that can hang with us and feel comfortable. Jamie fit in like no one had before. The next day, I had my jeweler put a ring together. I put the ring in a small box and I bought Jamie a coat. I placed the ring in the pocket of the coat. My brother and my parents were there when I gave Jamie her new coat. She put it on and loved it. I told her that there was something in the pocket. Jamie stuck her hand in the pocket. When she opened the box, she just stared at me. Shane's jaw dropped. Mom and Dad looked as happy as any two parents could have been. I don't think I even proposed. I blurted out, "You are going to marry me, aren't you?"

> When she opened the box, she just stared at me. Shane's jaw dropped. Mom and Dad looked as happy as any two parents could have been. I don't think I even proposed. I blurted out, "You are going to marry me, aren't you?"

I was ready to be engaged, but I was not ready to get married. I didn't really want to run from setting a date for any other reason except that I was not happy with myself. Dad told me years before that people get married at a high point or a low point in their lives. My marriage was not going to be at a low point. I wanted to get married when I was riding in the perfect wake and everything was crystal clear. We both hit the road in 2000 and we were determined to make the Finals. When it became apparent that we would make the Finals, we set a wedding date. Jamie and I made the 2000 NFR and we were married on April 21, 2001.

The Steiner family, including my daughter, Steely, after the 2002 Finals.

The wedding took place on the ranch in Bastrop. The guest list approached five hundred. Shane was my best man. Shane and I rode our Harleys up the lane that served as our outdoor "aisle." As we pulled up to the house, Shane stopped at the crossroad. "Bro," he said, "we can turn right and head to Mexico, or we can turn left to the wedding. I'll ride with you either way." Shane's timing on big issues has always been a little suspect. When I pointed left, he let me know it was a good call. Hey, isn't this why you need a good best man? Jamie arrived in a white horse-drawn carriage covered in flowers. Our pastor and good friend, Ray Burchette, performed the ceremony. He had married my parents 28 years ago. Burchette has always been there for our family in good times and bad.

Our daughter, Steely, was born in January 2002. Rocker Shane, our son, was born in December 2003. We wanted to have kids early. At the beginning of this chapter I discussed my wish to be able to relate to my own children, but there is another reason I wanted to have children while I was young: I want my kids to know their grandparents well. When I start coaching my kids in sports, I am going to need an assistant coach for Steely and Rocker. I know of no better candidate than my dad, and my mom will still make a beautiful cheerleader. What greater gift can a son or daughter give his or her parents than a grandchild?

I went to my 10-year high school reunion recently. Somebody at the reunion asked me about having kids. They wanted to know how my life had changed and what effect my daughter and new son have had on me. The first part of the question appeared to be rather obvious to me. Children change your life in the most fundamental ways. They wake up at all hours of the night and they want something. Sometimes, they are just scared and need to be held. These babies produce endless messy diapers and someone has to change them and make them all fresh again. However, most of the time I am not that someone. They still know that I am there for them, always. The second part of the question was more profound. What effect have my children had on me? I looked at my ex-classmate and answered very clearly.

"If a bullet was shot through this room and was heading for you, I am not at all certain that I would get in the way of it. I would consider the matter, but I cannot for certain give you an honest answer. On the other hand, if a bullet were headed for my daughter or my son, I would jump in front of it without hesitation. That's love you cannot put into words. I would gladly accept all the pain that my children may find in their lives."

# 11

# The NFR, Rounds Five and Six, 2002

Slim Shady had passed the test; he had done well in the fourth round. Now, my mindset was to stay on Shady. I needed to stay in the average hunt, but I also needed to win a round or two before the Finals ended. Shady could make that happen. I had placed in the first four rounds. I was talking to Dad every day about each round. We discussed what steer I needed and which ones I needed to stay away from. Dad never preached about what to do at the Finals. He knew that I was focused and he could tell by the look in my eyes that I wasn't there to celebrate just making the Finals this time.

The steer I had drawn for the fifth round wasn't great. No one had placed on the steer in the previous four rounds. With 10 rounds in the Finals, the worst thing I could have done was to get greedy. I couldn't try to win a round on a steer that I knew wasn't a go-round steer.

I had my hair cornrowed, or "bolted up" as they say, before the fifth round. It took almost an hour to do my hair. I firmly believe that individuals perform better when they look good or they feel like they look good. I was all Red-Bulled up

> **I firmly believe that individuals perform better when they look good or they feel like they look good.**

and I was on Slim Shady. To me, it didn't get any better than that. The mid-week crowds at the Finals started to get the buzz going about who was in position to win it all. There were no pretenders from that point on.

I backed Shady into the box. Everything happened really fast on that night. The steer settled in the chute and I nodded. I almost missed my steer. I thought the steer had gotten out behind Alfalfa, and Shady ran wide. I had to leap for the steer. I caught him and threw him in 4.3 seconds. The run was good for fifth place, but doubt crept into my mind about Shady. After I threw the steer in the fifth round, I got up and threw a handful of dirt in the general direction of the steer. I was pissed. Rod Lyman wound up winning the round. Bryan Fields and Luke Branquinho tied for second. Todd Suhn placed fourth, and I stayed in the

I went with the corn rows—and plenty of Red Bull—for the fifth round, but my horse troubles were beginning to get me down. (Photo courtesy of Mike Copeman Photography)

money at fifth. Birch Neggard finished sixth. Cash Myers and K. C. Jones did not place in the fifth round. My position was still good. It didn't matter: I was still pissed.

If I don't feel comfortable about something, then it always seems to go south. The doubts in my mind about Shady during the fifth round convinced me to go back to Boss. I had met a vet during the Finals named Greg Venaclausen. I talked to Dr. V the morning after the fifth round and told him that Boss was lame. He told me not to worry and suggested that we block Boss's front feet. The effect was similar to Novocain. The horse would not feel the pain in his foot. The vet said that the injury was just a bruise, so it would not get any worse. Everyone agreed with me at the time: if I had no confidence in Shady, then the smart thing to do was to get back on Boss. When the vet assured me that Boss would run without pain, I made the decision to get back on him.

**Everyone agreed with me at the time: if I had no confidence in Shady, then the smart thing to do was to get back on Boss.**

The steer I drew for the sixth round was a big steer that no one had done well through the first five rounds. This steer was one of those that didn't fit my style. I pulled Boss into the box and waited. When I nodded for the steer, I felt that Boss didn't explode from the box. I felt like my hand dropped all the way to my saddle horn before Boss left the box—he was really slow to take off. I knew Boss wasn't right, but I was trying to give him the benefit of the doubt. I couldn't keep switching horses. I caught my steer and threw him in 4.9 seconds.

The sixth round was the first round that I had not placed in the money. Rod Lyman won the round—his second go-round win in a row. Birch Neggard took second place, and Cash Myers finished sixth. The race to the title was still wide open. I wasn't freaked out about giving up a round, but I was having horse problems and that had me worried. I knew that my horse was not 100 percent, and that is not the mindset you want going into the final four rounds of the NFR.

The Finals were taking shape. After six rounds, there were seven contestants still in the hunt for the world championship. Cash Myers, Bill Pace, K. C. Jones, Birch Neggard, Lee Graves, Todd Suhn, and I had legitimate shots to win the world title.

# 12

# Life on the Water

In 1982 the Steiner Rodeo Company was sold. Dad sold everything associated with the rodeo company except one bull. The bull was the 1981 and 1982 bull of the year, Savage Seven. S7, as we called him, was a product of Mrs. Savage. Mrs. Savage had a ranch in Bay City, Texas, and once a year she would round up all her bulls and call Dad to come pick out the ones he wanted. We kept him as the only link to the Steiner Rodeo Company, but eventually Dad sold S7 and bought a boat.

We named the boat *Savage 7*. It was a Sea Ray. Dad had skied quite a bit when he was growing up and he slalom skied beautifully. I sat in the back of the boat and watched my dad water-ski and couldn't take my eyes off him.

When Shane and I were five and six, we started to get up on two skis. I took to it quickly, but two skis did not do anything for me. On Father's Day in 1982, we had our boat out and I decided that I wanted to learn to slalom that day. I couldn't get up on a small slalom ski, so I asked Dad if I could use his ski. Dad didn't think that was such a good idea because the ski was way too big for me. He let me try it anyway. When I got right up, Dad couldn't believe his eyes. That was my Father's Day present to my dad. I rode that one ski all over the lake that day.

Dad was thrilled, but he wasn't about to let the little brother show up the older brother. Shane didn't really care, but Dad insisted on Shane learning to slalom as soon as I proved that I could do it. Dad told Shane that we would stay out on the lake all night if we had to, but Shane was going to learn how to slalom. Shane rolled his eyes at me as if to say thanks a lot. Well, Shane got it pretty quickly, and we took to the water as often as we could from that day on.

Dad had a friend whose daughter skied for the University of Texas ski team. Cindy Present was a ski rat on Lake Austin from the time she was a toddler. Her boyfriend at the time, now her husband, also skied for the UT ski team. Cindy and Steve Present were slalom skiers and they put up a slalom ski course on Lake Austin. Dad started skiing with them, and before too long, Shane and I were dragging our skis down to the water at 5:00 A.M. every morning. We had our own private ski instructors. Shane and I got pretty good, so we started competing at the local level.

At that time, Cindy and Steve were performing at SeaWorld. They were doing trick skiing and jumping. Dad had promised to take Shane and me jumping. When we got to the water and watched Dad jump, I had to try it. I put the two jump skis and the jump suit on, and Dad put his arm around me. He told me that if I came around the turn and the

> **On Father's Day in 1982, we had our boat out and I decided that I wanted to learn to slalom that day.**

jump looked too big, then I should pull out and he wouldn't be disappointed at all. I really didn't think much about it then, but when I made that turn and caught a glimpse of that five-foot jump, it looked like I was skiing into a 10-foot wall! I immediately thought of Dad's offer to pull out. No way, I thought. I was going to show him that I wasn't scared to take that jump.

I hit the jump and it felt like I flew like a falcon. I hit my butt on the water and fell, but it didn't hurt at all. I jumped four or five more times, but I didn't ride one out. I had a blast. I jumped into the boat and started screaming about how cool that was. Dad was excited and I was thrilled.

I looked over at Shane, and he had a towel over his head. If a kid had ever wanted to disappear, that kid would have been Shane. Dad looked at Shane and asked, "You ready?"

Shane didn't answer. Dad pulled the towel off his head, and I swear to this day, Shane was as white as a ghost. Shane looked right through me. I could feel his glare. Shane put the skis on and we drove the boat around to the jump. Shane hit on his butt on the first jump, but landed his second jump and skied out of it. He turned out to be a much better jumper than I am, and he even wound up winning some jump tournaments. The next intriguing aspect of waterskiing was barefoot skiing.

We had seen Steve Present barefoot-ski a few times. We had been told the best way to start barefoot skiing was to sit on a kneeboard with your feet in the water in front of you. Let the boat pull you as fast as the boat could go, and when your butt couldn't take anymore, stand up and barefoot away. Shane was the one who first asked if we should try barefoot skiing. Dad agreed and off we went. Of course, everyone looked at me when the time came to try it. I didn't care. By now, though, we had a competition ski boat—no slow-ass Sea Ray. Our boat could push 45 miles per hour.

The first time I got in the water to barefoot, I positioned myself on the kneeboard. The boat took off, and I got up for about 10 seconds. It was a rush, but then I hit the water at 40-plus miles per hour and I rolled and flipped about 10 or 20 times. I did this a few times. Shane tried and pretty much did the same thing. We had a blast, but we were starting to get beat up.

Barefoot waterskiing on Lake Austin in 1988.

Finally, Dad brought Steve Present with us one day. Dad wanted to show him how we could barefoot for those short bursts. With Present in the boat, I got up for my 10 seconds and then took my beating. Present asked my dad if he could drive the boat. When he took the controls and I got in position to barefoot, he let up on the throttle to 30 miles per hour. I got up barefoot and stayed up all around the lake. I skied until I simply got tired. Shane did the same thing. The whole thing was a trip. We all got very good at it.

By the time I got to high school, Dad had taught all our friends to barefoot and slalom. Between two-a-day football practices, Dad would drive us all down to the lake and we would ski for a couple hours. My friends and Shane's friends were skiing addicts. Shane and I learned how to barefoot ski with one foot and do tumble turns and other barefoot tricks.

My brother and I took full advantage of our aquatic talents. Living next to the water was like having a free lifetime pass to an amusement park next to your house. We had a tree swing set up on a tree some 30 feet above the lake. The lake was the gathering place for Shane and me and all our friends. We had constant contests to see who could launch themselves farther out into the lake. In high school, when I got into trouble and Dad grounded me from going to Austin and hanging out with friends, he didn't ground me from the lake. I hopped on my jet ski and I was gone. In retrospect, Dad knew that I would find a way to get out, so he enabled me to think that I had to endure some vague form of punishment. The water almost felt like part of our home, so I was still confined to our property. It really didn't matter that the property extended the length of the Colorado River.

About the time that I started to rodeo in 1995, wake-boarding started to get popular. The boards were first called skurfers. They were like mini surfboards. The next year, the boards got streamlined, and wakeboarders were born. I took to wake-boarding, and in less than a month, I had conquered a flip from the water. I started

> **By the time I got to high school, Dad had taught all our friends to barefoot and slalom.**

doing front rolls, tantrums, flips, back rolls, and air raleys. Shane never got into wake-boarding like I did. I watched films of the pros, and I studied their tricks. I never got as good as a pro, but I got to where I could be considered an outlaw rider, which is just below the pro level. I even entertained thoughts of becoming a professional wake-boarder. There was a time (there were many times), when I decided to quit the rodeo business. I was in a prolonged slump and decided to take a crack at wake-boarding. I figured that wake-boarding would be an exciting way to make a living. I made Jamie drive me around the lake like a crazy person. Every missed flip or missed trick and I was yelling at Jamie. I blamed her for not driving the boat right. I was shocked that Jamie didn't leave me in the middle of the lake on countless occasions. I was practicing like I practiced rodeo. I was a fanatic. After three or four months of killing myself and driving Jamie crazy, I came to the conclusion that wake-boarding was not going to be my salvation. Hell, I never had so many physical injuries in my life. I messed up my shoulder, had stitches in my head, and pounded my body from the height and speed of the tricks. Wake-boarding sent me back into rodeo.

**I took to wake-boarding, and in less than a month, I had conquered a flip from the water. I started doing front rolls, tantrums, flips, back rolls, and air raleys.**

Skiing and water sports in general have been a great training ground for rodeo. The constant pulling of a rope has developed my back muscles in obvious ways. The continuous pulling over the years combined strength with balance, two things essential in bull-dogging. The motion and action of your feet in barefoot skiing are identical to the footwork in bulldogging.

I remember in 1995 I brought Todd Fox to the lake and introduced him to barefoot skiing. He watched me at first and was amazed. He was somewhat hesitant about partic-ipating in a sport that could jeopardize his income if he got hurt, but I convinced him to try it. He picked it up like he was born to barefoot. He explained that the motion and footwork was identical to sliding a steer. I went out and bought a dummy steer's head like the ones they stick in the hay to teach roping. I removed the prongs from the back of the head and brought it to the lake. I used the steer's head as my pull rope. I would barefoot-ski while holding onto the steer's head. I would bring the steer's head down low or practice catching the head up high while I was sliding on the water in the perfect replica of sliding along the arena floor. I incorporated many aspects of barefoot skiing into my rodeo mechanics. I always had good feet when I caught my steers. Even in the mud, I had a solid foundation.

Over the years, I have had many people join me on the water. Todd Fox was a frequent visitor. Frank Davis came down quite a bit. Olie Davis, a good friend from Del Rio, Texas, was a big, 270-pound bulldogger who looked like a giant marlin on the water. Bryan Fields took his turn on the water. Eight-time World Champion Calf Roper Joe Beaver has been a regular on the water with his son Brodie. I taught Brodie how to wake-board, and he took right to it. Ross Coleman, Cory Melton, and some fellow bull riders from the Professional Bull Riders (PBR) have been down to visit. Coleman is a good friend, and the bull riders were nuts. They all got up on the boom and began to barefoot right away. The bull riders complained the next day about how sore they were, but they loved it. These guys made their living bouncing on the backs of 2,000-pound freight trains, but they got sore from barefoot skiing. They told me that next to riding a bull, the barefoot skiing thing could be a terrific female magnet.

# 13

## The NFR, Rounds Seven and Eight, 2002

By the seventh round, I was still unhappy about the uncertainty surrounding my horses. In my mind, I was still convinced that Shady ran wide in the fifth round, and I was afraid if he did that again, I would miss my steer. The vet assured me that Boss would run fine with his front feet numb.

The steer I had drawn for the seventh round was a big, flat-headed steer and for sure not the one I wanted. Now, I was beginning to get a little frustrated. I wanted to win some go-rounds. I was a gambler and liked to push the envelope. Everyone was telling me how well I was doing in the average title race, but I needed to win some rounds. I didn't want to leave it all on the average.

When I pulled Boss into the box for the seventh round, the crowd at the Thomas and Mack was pumped. When I called for the steer, I released my hand and Boss hesitated. I had to kick him to get him started. I had a really good run and threw my steer in five seconds flat, but that time didn't allow me to place in the round. Bill Pace, K. C. Jones, Cash Myers, Birch Neggard, and Todd Suhn had better times than I did. There was a logjam for the title after the seventh round.

Boss wasn't running, and I couldn't get him to fire out of the box. I caught my steer at the back end of the arena. If you have ever run a steer at the Thomas and Mack, you would know how scary that is. Just ask Byron Walker.

I decided that I needed to work Boss, and he would be fine. I found my friend Charlie Horky Thursday night after the rodeo. He team ropes and has a full-sized arena just outside the Las Vegas city limits. I told him that I needed a place to work my horse and make some adjustments. Charlie was great; he said that he would have the steers penned in the morning, and my driver, Whip, knew how to get to his ranch.

The next morning, Butch Stokes came into town. Stokes and I had breakfast and he told me that I needed to take both horses out that morning. He told me that we needed to make some adjustments to Slim Shady's tie-down (the rope that prevents the horse from coming up too fast). When we got to Horky's ranch, I got on Shady first. It was the morning of the eighth round and I was still confused about which horse to ride. Butch took Shady's tie-down up a few holes, and I rode him in the box. I wanted to run past a steer, just to see how Shady would react. Boom, Shady could have run over that steer. He exploded out of the box and I ran him a few more times. That horse fired out of the box every time. Then, I got

**It was the morning of the eighth round and I was still confused about which horse to ride.**

on Boss. I couldn't do anything on Boss. He loped out of the box and everything I tried, failed.

Now, it was time to decide. Butch, my dad, Jamie, and I sat down to figure this thing out. It seemed like a board of directors meeting at IBM. Butch told me that if I rode Shady with his tie-down adjusted, he thought I would win two of the next three rounds. Jamie agreed, and that was something because she never fully agrees with anyone. I was sure that Butch must have been on to something. Dad felt that Butch had the best handle on the matter and that I should run with Shady. It was very unusual for anyone to be swapping horses at this point of the NFR: imagine a Super Bowl team switching quarterbacks on every set of downs. Luckily, sending in my backup was like sending in Brett Favre.

On Friday night in Vegas, my brother Shane arrived in town. He was headlining at the Orleans Hotel on Friday and Saturday nights. I knew that I would be introducing him on stage. There were countless executives in town to see him perform. There were sponsors in town to check out potential new clients. There were people from Levi Strauss. All the Wrangler reps were in Vegas. They were all coming to the rodeo.

We had more friends in town than any other night. I was back on Shady. It was the bottom of the ninth, two outs, bases loaded, and I was up. It was a big night for our family. I have never been an overly religious person, but I said a prayer that night. I didn't want to be selfish, but I wanted the evening to work out for all of us.

I drew the steer I had wanted all week. This steer had a lot of action and definitely fit me. The faster things happened, the better I liked it. I hated slow starts, slow steers, and slow finishes. Dad was nervous about the draw and he kept reminding me to let the steer move far enough so that I wouldn't break the barrier. I wasn't ever known for my good scoring ability, but I knew the start in Vegas. Once I got on Shady for the eighth round, all my fears vanished. I was ready to rock and roll.

I was up fourth in the round. I slid Shady back into the box and waited for him to settle. I had two good friends, Mack Altizer and Herbert Theriot, to hold Shady in the corner so he couldn't spin out. I called for the steer and Shady shot out of the box. I threw the steer in 3.6

I was back on Shady for the eighth round, and we nailed it. (Photo courtesy of Mike Copeman Photography)

seconds. The Thomas and Mack exploded. I kicked up some dirt and raised my arms. I remember screaming something like, "Bring it on!" I knew that I had delivered with the bases loaded.

**It was very unusual for anyone to be swapping horses at this point of the NFR: imagine a Super Bowl team switching quarterbacks on every set of downs. Luckily, sending in my backup was like sending in Brett Favre.**

The only problem now was that I had to sit through 11 other bulldoggers. My palms were sweating while I waited through the eighth round. Luke Branquinho's and Jason Lahr's scores were both 3.7 seconds and they tied for second place. Joey Bell got a 3.9 for fourth place. Before the eighth round, Mom had asked me what we were going to do if I won the round. The buckle presentation at the Gold Coast Hotel and Shane's show at the Orleans were going on at the same time. I kissed my mother on the cheek and told her that would be a wonderful problem to have. As I sat behind the box and watched the remaining bulldoggers go, I thought about that problem and prayed for the chance to solve it. Dad called the Gold Coast Hotel and asked if they would change the buckle presentation order. Each night of the NFR, the go-round winner in each event is given a shitty

After the eighth round, I rode my chopper onstage at the Orleans Hotel to introduce Shane, who also nailed it. The stars were aligned for the Steiners that night.

buckle at the Gold Coast Hotel. They agreed to give out my buckle last. That gave us time to go to Shane's show.

I had brought my chopper to Vegas. It was there for publicity, but I also rode it almost every day to get a massage. I was asked to be the MC at Shane's show. The announcer at the Orleans came over the speakers and introduced Tommy Shane Steiner's brother, steer wrestler Sid Steiner. The lights were down and they played the old Steppenwolf song, "Born to Be Wild." I rode my chopper up on the stage and introduced my brother. I talked about Shane for a few minutes and then brought him out. Shane broke right into a song entitled, "That Just Wouldn't Be Me," which was the perfect theme song for the way my brother lives his life. The night could not have gone any better. Shane sounded fantastic. I listened to a couple of songs from backstage, then went out to the main seating because the sound was so much

> **The announcer at the Orleans came over the speakers and introduced Tommy Shane Steiner's brother, steer wrestler Sid Steiner. The lights were down and they played the old Steppenwolf song, "Born to Be Wild." I rode my chopper up on the stage and introduced my brother.**

better from in front. Shane kicked ass and we all hopped into the limo for the ride back to the Gold Coast.

At the Gold Coast, they introduced the whole family. Shane, Jamie, Steely, Mom, and Dad were all brought up on stage with me to receive my buckle for winning the eighth round. I haven't hit 30 yet, but I cannot imagine many better moments than we had that night. Some nights the stars line up right. As my dad told me, we caught some magic that night. Luckily for me, I didn't let it go until I left Las Vegas. On Friday the 13th, 2002, my stars didn't just line up; they stood at attention and never broke ranks.

# 14

# The Rodeo Life

My wife and I now have two children. I certainly want them to be able to take care of themselves. I know that my daughter, Steely, has inherited a tenacious independence from Jamie and me. There will always be those agonizing hurdles that all children must face. Initially, the hurdles are walking for the first time or riding a bike for the first time. Going to school for the first time or getting on a horse for the first time can be tough days, but we all got through it.

Jamie and I will watch and worry like every parent does when our children go to school for the first time. As parents, we all hope that our kids enjoy their new surroundings and make new friends. Steely and Rocker will enjoy every opportunity to learn and grow in a safe environment. But, if there is a bully first grader stalking the playground and that bully sets his sights on my daughter or my son, then I want my kids to be able to take care of business.

I was a late bloomer in high school. I didn't pick up any real size until my junior and senior years in high school. I wouldn't say that I was unusually small in high school, but I had to find the weight room and open an account at GNC to push 200 pounds. I distinctly remember asking Dad about fighting when I was young. I was worried that I wouldn't be as tough as Dad and I wouldn't be able to stand up for myself. He just told me that I had enough Steiner in me and not to worry. For some reason, that always stuck with me.

Contrary to what you may now believe, rodeo is not all about busting it up inside and outside of the arena. The business of rodeo is grueling and long. The season runs almost 12 months per year: the NFR is concluded during the second week of December, and the first big rodeo of the next year is in mid-January. Everyone hits Denver to start the year off right.

All of the competitors seem to be split into three groups. The northern group comes from Montana, Wyoming, Utah, and Colorado. There are the southern guys from Oklahoma and Texas, and then you have the California guys. Don't let anyone try to tell you that when you have made the NFR and your state is about to be called in the Grand Entry, you don't get goose bumps when you follow your flag into the arena. Travel bonds are formed in rodeo based on the geographic boundaries of the cowboys' home states. The PRCA schedule follows geographic regions as the year progresses. Winter, spring, and summer rodeos can be organized by regions, with some exceptions.

**I wouldn't say that I was unusually small in high school, but I had to find the weight room and open an account at GNC to push 200 pounds.**

After Denver, the rodeo tour comes to Texas for stops in San Antonio, Houston, and Fort Worth. Imagine the guys from Canada or northern Montana coming to Texas. They basically have to spend the better part of two months in Texas, given the dates of the three big Texas rodeos. There are some California rodeos in the spring that I made a point to hit. When the summer started, it became a free-for-all. Reno, Nevada, kicked off the summer rodeo binge in late June. Greeley followed Reno, and the Fourth of July run began.

As a competitor, you had to hit as many rodeos over the weekend of July fourth as you could. We could go to Pecos, New Mexico; Prescott, Arizona; Window Rock, Arizona; St. Paul, Oregon; Eugene, Oregon; Alberta, Canada; Springdale, Arizona; or a thousand other spots. Cody, Wyoming, was a one-head rodeo (one with only one performance per rider, with the best time winning) that paid $10,000. Hard to miss that one. You had to give yourself a chance to run one steer for 10 grand. We had to figure out the rodeos that offered the most money and that were close enough together to make it possible to hit them all. Most of the travel was done in chartered planes. I hated small planes. I did not like bouncing between mountains in a thunderstorm with a pilot I barely knew. I liked my feet to be on the ground.

**Don't let anyone try to tell you that when you have made the NFR and your state is about to be called in the Grand Entry, you don't get goose bumps when you follow your flag into the arena.**

After the Fourth of July weekend, almost everyone went to Canada for Calgary. Salinas, California; Salt Lake City, Utah; and Cheyenne, Wyoming, followed. The northwest run was pretty much the rest of the summer. The fall run brought you back to New Mexico and California. There were also rodeos in Arkansas and Tennessee. The nerves started cracking in the fall with the NFR standings, and everyone was making one last burst to make the Finals or solidify their spots.

The long rodeo seasons had been the backdrop to countless Chris LeDoux songs and too many broken relationships. After months on the road, you forgot what your family looked like. There were spots in my schedules when I had been on the road for four months. When I started competing, I would go home whenever I wanted. After a couple of years, I stopped doing that. When I was on the road, I was focused. When I went home, I had a good time, partied with all my friends, slept in my own bed, ate good meals, and got comfortable. Then I had to go back on the road and it took me another two weeks to get back into it and get my focus back. Rodeo was a commitment on all fronts. To be successful in rodeo, you had to travel most of the year. It was that simple.

Another factor that is often overlooked is the danger in rodeo travel. My desire to retire from competition after winning a title grew from many factors, not the least of which was the uncertainty of traveling unknown highways at 3:00 in the morning and being dead tired. I know how dangerous it is to have someone driving that is tired. I have been in the back of the truck trying to get some sleep and I know that at such times your life is in someone else's hands, and you have little or no control on how it turns out. I do not want my children's future to be dictated by a casual friend that fell asleep at the wheel. Many more cowboys have died on the way to the rodeo than at the rodeo. That is why I called my parents all the time. Mom and Dad knew the drill. They were champion rodeo competitors and had to travel like the rest of us. I often called

Mom at 4:00 in the morning to tell her that I arrived in one piece. I knew Mom would be up watching the weather in the areas that I was traveling in. My call would allow her to get some sleep. I don't want that for Jamie, Steely, and Rocker. When Steely and Jamie were traveling with me, it became very unnerving. Every time we hit a bump, I would jump up and check out who was driving and make sure he was awake.

**Rodeo was a commitment on all fronts. To be successful in rodeo, you had to travel most of the year. It was that simple.**

From the time Jamie and I were together through the 2002 Finals, we were lucky enough to have a home to stay at during the northwest rodeo runs. Jamie's mom lived in Washington, and during the northwest run, we stayed with her in Kennewick. They had stalls for the horses, and at least we felt like we had some roots during the season. When everyone else was still camping and sleeping in motel rooms, I had a familiar place to go back to. It really helped.

The downtime in rodeo was what I had a hard time with. I wasn't very good at just sitting around. Some guys liked sitting around a hotel room watching *SportsCenter*. I had to get out. I wanted to go play golf or basketball, lift weights, see a movie, or even go miniature golfing. Bryan Fields and I got along great while we were partners on the road. We did everything together. Sleepy was agreeable to any activity. We often sought out the closest gym or health club. I could sweet-talk just about any female health club attendant into allowing us to work out for free. I liked to think everyone else was sitting around watching television and I was busting my ass in a weight room. Reward and sacrifice were how I based my travels. If I didn't do well in the rodeo, then I didn't go out. I knew so many guys that went out to the bars every night after a perf, whether they did well or stunk up the joint. If I did poorly, then I needed to punish myself. If I did well, then I was the first one to the local watering hole.

Rodeo was like high school. When you were the new kid on the block, everyone had to take their pokes and feel you out. No one was going to give you a place in the sport. You have to go and take your place in any sport, but especially rodeo. There are no contracts in rodeo. If we didn't ride well or we didn't throw our steers, then we didn't get paid. A quarterback can have a bad game or two and he will still get paid. A baseball player can have a bad year and he still gets paid. That does not happen in rodeo. If we do not perform, then we don't make squat.

In 1998, I was still fairly new on the circuit. I had been tested a few times and more than held my own against some guys looking to find out what Sid Steiner was made of. Shane had called me and asked how things were going on the road. I asked him if he would come out and spend the weekend with me at Cheyenne. Cheyenne was a cool rodeo and I missed my brother. Shane planned to fly out as soon as he finished a singing gig. He dressed wild in the early days of his singing career. On this trip, the airlines had lost his luggage, and he was left with the clothes on his back.

> # There are no contracts in rodeo. If we didn't ride well or we didn't throw our steers, then we didn't get paid.

The shirt Shane was wearing on the night he arrived was like a neon billboard—not at all the way to slip in unnoticed at a cowboy bar. On Shane's first night in Cheyenne, we went to the Hitching Post, a tavern that has played host to most of the cowboys competing at "the daddy of 'em all."

Shane and I were sitting at the bar and he had his wild shirt on. It didn't bother me and I didn't care if it bothered anyone else. Ty Murray was in the bar with a few guys.

"Well, there's a shirt for your ass," Ty Murray announced after Shane's shirt had garnered some attention.

I was about to say something back, but Shane told me to let it go. He was right. After all, it was Ty Murray, and he didn't know me at all. I respected the hell out of Murray. He is a true cowboy and turned out to be one of the guys I respect the most. He loved the old cowboy traditions, and he had earned the right to hold onto his ways. His

Shane and I proved we could take care of ourselves one night in Cheyenne. I guess drinking and fighting are just byproducts of rodeo life.

accomplishments in rodeo were second to none. Well, Murray went about his business, but some bronc riders couldn't leave it alone. There had always been a natural rivalry between roughstock cowboys and timed-event cowboys. When the conversation finally got around to Shane's gender identification, then it was time to figure this thing out. One of the bronc riders kept staring at Shane. I finally asked him if he had a problem. He wanted to know if my brother was gay. His problem had to be addressed immediately. I hit that guy hard, and Shane stood up and punched another guy. We stood back to back for a few minutes throwing punches. By the time the bouncers made their way through the tussle, there were a few guys down. Shane and I were still standing. I looked around and stood up on a stool and asked if anyone else had a problem with my brother.

Ty Murray stood up and yelled, "I love him."

They asked us all to leave that bar and we walked next door to another bar. Murray came up to me and asked if he could buy us a beer. He wanted

> I respected the hell out of Murray. He is a true cowboy and turned out to be one of the guys I respect the most.

to make sure that we were friends. That night, Shane and I spent some quality time with a quality guy. Ty Murray is a supercool person that I now consider a good friend. When I see him, he always refers to the night in Cheyenne as the night when Shane and I cleared the bar. I would hang with Ty Murray any day or night.

After that night, I never had many problems with rodeo guys. All I ever wanted to do was to let people know that I would stand up for myself. That's all. I didn't want to be the toughest guy in rodeo. I knew that I wasn't, but I never set out to prove that I was.

I didn't set out to get in a fight that night, but there is no better feeling than *mano a mano*. Somebody wins and somebody loses. If those words sound like outdated testosterone rhetoric to some, then those individuals have never been in a fight. Those individuals have never listened to a tape of Vince Lombardi talking about conflict and victory. There is a line from the movie *Fight Club* that says it perfectly: "How much can you know about yourself if you've never been in a fight?" It is impossible to know what you are made of until you are tested.

I may be a little corny, but I often see and hear things that give me goose bumps. I remember a quote from General Patton that I thought was great. Patton once said, "I fight where I am told, and I win where I fight."

# 15

# The NFR, Round Nine, 2002

I sat with my family at the Orleans after the buckle ceremony ended at the Gold Coast on Friday night. We were drinking some beer and it was getting late. I could not have scripted the night to go any better, but I wasn't done. The night flew by and before I could soak it all in, the focus became the ninth round. I noticed Dad looking at me. He didn't have to say anything because I knew what he was thinking.

I told Dad that I was right where I wanted to be. I think Dad was trying to gauge my nerves. He wasn't expecting me to get a case of the jitters, but he wanted me to know that he was there for me no matter what happened.

I knew that I was third in the average with two rounds to go. I had won a lot of money already, and I was in a position to win a world title. If I drew any kind of decent steers, I had a shot. That was all I could ask for with two rounds to go at the National Finals. The exact order of the competitors was damned near impossible to know at that point. In other words, going into the ninth round, I didn't know if I was in second place, third place, or fourth place. There were so many scenarios that could have presented themselves during the ninth and tenth rounds. Money won during the year was added to money won during each go-round and the average money. That total determined the eventual champion. Four of us had a shot at the title. Nothing was settled yet, but I was in a good position.

I told Dad that if nothing went off the deep end, the real deal would come down to the 10th round. Dad told me that he had complete confidence in my ability to handle the pressure. That's what being a Steiner was all about. I knew that Cash Myers was winning the average and he was the main man to beat with two rounds to go.

Jamie went down to exercise Shady on Saturday morning. She noticed a lump on his front tendon. Jamie thought, here we go again, but the problem never really materialized. Shady seemed fine, and the lump probably came from some scar tissue that aggravated the tendon. Regardless, Shady was my horse for the last two rounds.

The ninth-round steer that I drew was nothing special. He was not going to win me the go-round. The steer ran a little, but he wasn't horrible either. He was just what I needed: a shot at the 10<sup>th</sup> round and the world title. I knew that Rod Lyman and Joey Bell were out of the average race. I was in fourth place without the average money, so I knew that I had a good position. I figured that the race was between four guys: Cash Myers, K. C. Jones, Bill Pace, and me.

In the ninth round, I placed sixth for a check. I walked away from the steer after my four-second time was posted. There were no hysterical gyrations or fist-pumping displays

The ninth round was all about just staying in position to make something happen in the final round. I just went about my business and saved everything for last. (Photo courtesy of Mike Copeman Photography)

after my run. I just wanted to get it done and give myself a chance in the 10th round. I had done that.

**There were no hysterical gyrations or fist-pumping displays after my run. I just wanted to get it done and give myself a chance in the 10th round. I had done that.**

Dreams are funny things. Sometimes, they almost seem better when they are so far out of reach that there is little pressure to actually achieve the dream. The effort could always be true, and the quest could always appear noble and worthy of my dedication. The pressure didn't figure in until the whole dream was within reach. We didn't talk much about the final round during the evening. It was an early evening. The last perf was always held on Sunday afternoon. I was certain that no one wanted to upset me or jinx the outcome by telling me that I had a great shot at the title.

Las Vegas was not the most serene place on the planet to search for that inner peace that would have allowed you to perform outside the reach of the commotion surrounding you. I didn't care. I knew that there were some things that I could not control, but the things that I could were under control. I wanted to go for the round. I wanted one steer that would give me the round. All during the Finals, I had hoped to give myself a chance after the ninth round. Now that I had that chance, I wanted to blow past that finish line.

I could fight the urge to win the next round and play it safer. It would be safer to respect the barrier and not risk incurring the 10-second penalty. The smart thing would be to concentrate on all my fundamentals and stay in the hunt. Let the order fall out and put the pressure on someone else to falter.

Screw that! I was there to win it all and I wanted to seal the deal by winning the last round.

# 16

# One Brother

The sequence of chapters within this book obviously has some significance to my life, but it does not signify the order of importance regarding any member of my family. My entire family has played such an instrumental part in every aspect of my life that we have all become one, and each individual is no more or less important to the bond that makes our family. I have been blessed in many ways, but in no ways more evident than the people I call my family.

Mom and Dad could not have hired a screenwriter to script my life any better than the paths they provided. The only reservation that I have about my kids getting to know their grandparents so well is that Mom and Dad set the bar so damn high that I will be hard pressed to provide the encore. Some say parenting should be easier when you had the gold standard to watch for nearly 30 years. I'll find out pretty quickly.

I saved one of the last chapters for my brother, Shane. Growing up is a battle for knowledge, experiences, attention, mistakes, and maturity. I am certain that I would not have sailed through most of my toughest obstacles if my brother had not been with me. The whole is only as strong as the sum total of the parts. Shane has been my best friend since I was old enough to have a friend. When it's all said and done and they plant me somewhere in the Texas countryside, I will have known many people and had many friends, but I will have been lucky enough to have had four best friends. I trust my dad, my mom, Jamie, and Shane with everything I have, including my children. Your blood is what it's all about.

Shane and I are 14 months apart, and he's been my best buddy since day one.

It's hard to remember back to the rodeo company. Dad sold the Steiner Rodeo Company when Shane and I were really young. I know that we ran around the grounds of every rodeo looking for whatever trouble could be found. The cowboys facilitated in every way whatever schemes Shane and I cooked up. My clearest memories of my brother began at the lake ranch. Shane liked to control the action, and I was just happy to tag along. Hell, Shane was older and I knew that none of the kids my age could be any cooler than my older brother. That was never more evident than when we took possession of our first motorized vehicle, a red go-cart.

The *General Lee* was the name we assigned to the two-seat go-cart that Shane and I shared as miniature "Dukes." I remember Shane taking control even back then. He was 14 months older. We imagined ourselves as Bo and Luke Duke from the *Dukes of Hazzard* TV show. Every time I tried to drive the go-cart, Shane would holler out that I was Bo and Bo never drove. Luke was the driver and Shane was always Luke. I never did get to drive the *General Lee*. I recall riding shotgun all the time and yelling, "Yee-ha!" Even though I never got to drive, I loved riding in that go-cart. Shane could really drive.

Sports were a major focus in our lives. Sports were very important to Dad, and I loved every minute of the games and the practices. It would be fair to say that Shane was not as impassioned about team sports as I was. I enjoyed lifting weights with dad. I enjoyed all the baseball practices and football practices, but Shane didn't share my enthusiasm about those sports. In fact, years later, Shane confessed about how pissed off he used to get because I kept throwing gasoline into the fire on sports. If I did something, then Dad insisted that Shane do the same thing. I loved trying new sports and new tricks. It's not that Shane couldn't do the same things; he simply didn't care about doing them. The

**Growing up is a battle for knowledge, experiences, attention, mistakes, and maturity. I am certain that I would not have sailed through most of my toughest obstacles if my brother had not been with me.**

waterskiing was the perfect example. Shane was every bit as talented at the sport as I was, but his heart wasn't in it. He probably proved he was a better athlete than I was because Shane excelled at these sports without the enthusiasm that I brought to each outing. Shane's natural talent carried him through the sports. I remember when Mom told Dad one year that he was pushing Shane too hard at baseball. Mom said that he was only playing to please Dad. Dad thought that was BS. So one day when we were all riding in the Suburban, Dad decided to talk to Shane.

"Son," Dad began, "I don't want you playing baseball to please me. If you don't want to play baseball this year, then you don't have to play." Dad finished, confident that Shane would certainly choose to play.

"Thanks, Dad," Shane replied almost before Dad had completed his offer. "I don't want to play baseball this year."

You could see Dad fuming in the front seat, but he couldn't say anything. That was the last time he offered Shane a way out of any sport. The next year, Dad insisted that Shane play baseball. Dad figured that playing sports just for him was better than not playing at all.

Shane and I remained tight until he got his driver's license. It was very natural for an older brother to want some space from his younger brother. I wanted to go everywhere with Shane, but he didn't want his younger brother tagging along everywhere he went. I had a hard time with that for a long time. During high school we established our own set of friends, and I knew that I wanted to hang out with my big brother, but he preferred not to have a little brother tag along on weekends. I have never had a little brother, so I'm not certain how I would have handled the same circumstances, but I tried to get Shane to hang with me as much as possible. We always looked out for each other and never would have allowed anyone else to mess with the other, but high school was an equal-but-separate deal.

In football, I think I made things harder for Shane without realizing what I was doing. Coach Ray Dowdy was the perfect coach for me. I enjoyed the in-your-face attitude that Dowdy brought to our football team. Shane took things more personally and didn't care for coach Dowdy's screaming rants. Shane was a talented football player who struggled with his ability to enjoy the game. I hated scrimmages in practice when we went full speed. During my junior year, I had more problems at practice than any other year. I was first team defense, and Shane was first team offense. During defensive drills, Shane had to run scout team offense and simulate the opposing team's offensive style. We were told to tee off on the scout team. Shane was a running back and I was a linebacker. Coach Dowdy insisted that I nail my brother when the time came. I refused. The scout team offensive line was second string and the backs got killed. I told Coach that I was not going to go after my brother and that any sane coach should realize the potential damage from an injury under those circumstances. Coach Dowdy and I got into some seismic clashes regarding the way I hit my brother in practice. I didn't think we should be trying to kill each other as teammates, and I really had a problem with going after my brother.

When Shane graduated high school, he went to a small university in Austin called St. Edwards. Mom cried so hard when Shane left you would have thought he was going to

What they say is true: blood is thicker than water.

the marine corps boot camp in San Diego. He went to a school 20 minutes away. After my first football game during my senior year, I remember Shane showing up in the parking lot after the game. He asked if I wanted to hang out or go do something. That is what I always wanted. During the football season and my whole senior year, Shane would call during the week and we got to where we hung out all the time. I'm not sure what created the chance. It might have been that Shane moved out or he just grew up. I never did figure that out, but it didn't matter.

Music crept into Shane's life almost by the back door. In high school, Shane had a truck. When we would have to go to school, Shane would put on his full-length duster and head for the truck. No one could say that Shane was not an individual because he dressed the part in high school. The mornings may have been pretty cold, but I knew that by lunchtime the day would have warmed up. I didn't want to drag a coat around all day. So, no matter how cold it was in the morning, I hopped in the truck with a T-shirt and jeans on. We would get in the truck and Shane would take one look at me and smile. As soon as we left for school, he would roll all the windows down. I sat in the front seat and shivered. I begged him to close the windows. He would look at me and say, "You should have worn a coat, dude."

Pearl Jam would be blasting in the truck and Shane sang along with the music. I remember thinking then that my brother could sing. There was a song by Living Color called "Cult of Personality," a bad-ass rock song. Shane belted that song out on the way to school and he sounded better than the original band. That got me to thinking. Maybe this talent ran in the family. So, I put on that Living Color tune when I was alone and tried belting it out like Shane. I was terrible, and haven't gotten any better. We all knew that Dad could sing, so I asked if he'd ever heard Shane sing. He hadn't. When Dad made Shane sing, he was amazed. I think Dad was relieved to see that Shane did have a passion for something.

> **Coach Dowdy and I got into some seismic clashes regarding the way I hit my brother in practice. I didn't think we should be trying to kill each other as teammates, and I really had a problem with going after my brother.**

After Shane quit college, he went to work on the ranch. Shane had lasted about halfway through the first semester. He beat the hell out of my college career. Dad used to say that he must have had the two smartest kids in the country because one finished college in 10 weeks and the other finished in four days.

Dad had a cattle sale twice a year on the ranch. It was a big deal and they even hired a band to entertain the buyers. My parents asked Shane to get up and sing with the band.

This was Shane's first experience in front of a live audience. He sang well and the crowd loved him. Dad bought Shane a guitar right after that performance, and he picked it up faster than anyone thought possible. The bandleader was Bubba Cox, and he was so impressed with Shane that he offered him a chance to be their lead singer. Shane had long hair and gave the band a better connection to the younger audience. The band started playing at all the big country bars around Austin and the whole family always went to watch. Dad would pace around and could hardly enjoy the show. I used to ask Dad why he was so nervous. Shane could sing and it was not like he had a bad day singing, aside from forgetting the words to a song, his voice was going to sound great.

**Dad used to say that he must have had the two smartest kids in the country because one finished college in 10 weeks and the other finished in four days.**

Success dogged Shane and me almost as if we were a team. When good things happened to me, some good things always seemed to be happening to Shane. It's hard to put specific dates on everything, but my brother and I climbed different ladders to success at the same time. By the time I had made the NFR in 2000, Shane had signed his first record deal with RCA Records. On one particular night in Las Vegas during the 2000 NFR, Shane and I met up for a few beers after my round concluded. Shane had all his record guys around and they were pumped about an upcoming tour. I had just won a round and was about to receive a go-round buckle at the Gold Coast. Shane finished a beer and looked at me.

"Don't you think it's a little weird, what we're doing?" Shane asked me.

"What's weird?" I didn't know where he was going.

"We lost Teece last year. We struggled from 1995–1999. You broke more barriers over the last four years. I had to play more small clubs than you guys hit in an entire year on the road. Then in 1999 we lose Teece. This year, everything seems to be falling into place for both of us. Doesn't it seem like Teece is up there making something happen for us?" Shane looked out the windows of the Thomas and Mack. I smiled. He was right.

When people have gotten to know our family, I have heard them say many times that I am the spitting image of my father. Shane inherited much of my dad's free spirit. We all knew that Shane would walk down his own road, and in all likelihood, the road would follow some detours. Shane had told me on many occasions that he wanted to have kids eventually, but didn't necessarily want to be married. The worst thing to happen to anyone is to get into a relationship that they don't want to be in. Shane and I never felt any pressure to get married. I never would have gotten married just to please someone, but when I met Jamie, I knew that we were the best chance around to give Mom and Dad grandchildren. If I had never met Jamie, I'd probably still be single. Shane will know when and if the right person comes along. For now, Shane's family is growing just the same. My kids are Shane's kids. It's that simple.

I feel that it may be appropriate to address some concerns that have come up from time to time when people get to know my family and me. When Jim McMahon referred to individuality in the Foreword, he connected it with the automatic misconception that being different was negative. Many people have looked at rebellious attitudes and assumed the sources must have been born from anger and frustration. McMahon talked about the flawed perception that unconventional behavior means malicious behavior. Shane and I came from the best family environment that two boys could have experienced. Our desire to stand out and excel at what we do came from parents who didn't believe that ordinary was acceptable. My brother and I chose to be different—not because we were lashing out at the boundaries that were placed around us, but because of the endless opportunities that were put before us.

# 17

# The NFR, Round 10, 2002

"Catching the magic" is a saying that Dad, Shane, and I have used for a while now. It's about doing what it takes when the time is right. You get a few chances in life to do something great. When that time arises, you can't be afraid of failure. You have to reach out and *catch it*. Anyone that is great has let it slip by a time or two, but that comes with the territory. If you put yourself in enough big situations, you are bound to be let down at some point. But what doesn't kill you only makes you stronger.

I had let myself down in the 2000 Finals. Going into the ninth round, I was in great position to win a world title. To tell the truth, the pressure got to me and I missed my steer. I was determined to not let that happen again.

It was Sunday, December 15, 2002. On that cool Las Vegas afternoon, we were going to find out whether the stars were lined up for me. The superstitions became nerve-racking before the 10th round. No one wanted to be the one to break the good luck. Jamie insisted on pinning my contestant number on my back, the same way she had for each of the previous nine rounds. The shower routines stayed the same. The limo rides stayed the same. The music stayed the same. My two Red Bulls stayed the same. My dad's hot dog habits stayed the same, although if the Finals had gone on any longer, I think Dad would have shit-canned the hot dog tradition.

I grew up with a world champion for a dad. A world champion gave me a ride to baseball practice every day of my life. A world champion coached most of my teams when I was a kid. I had a world champion teach me how to stand up for myself, and I had a world champion teach me how to treat the most important people in my life. That always made me proud and I wanted that for my kids. The last round of the 2002 NFR was about to hand me that chance.

I "caught the magic" in the final round, and nothing felt better than taking that victory lap after eight years of hard work and endless travel. (Photo courtesy of Mike Copeman Photography)

I came into the Finals in seventh place. After nine rounds, there were eight bulldoggers separated by less than $13,000. Cash Myers came into the Finals in first place. After nine rounds, Cash stood in second place overall and first place in the average race. Luke Branquinho ranked first, but was out of the average. That would kick him out of the hunt for the title. I was in second place for the average title, barely one second behind Myers. That placed me somewhere near the top overall, second or third, I wasn't sure. I was a little disappointed after the ninth round. When I woke up Sunday morning, I knew that winning was all I cared about and nothing else would be acceptable. Second place was not an option for me.

I talked to Dad before the steers were drawn and told him that I needed to win the 10th round. I told him that I needed the same steer that Joey Bell missed and Bill Pace and K. C. Jones won a round with. Dad didn't want anything to do with that steer. Dad told me that if I finished third on Sunday afternoon and Cash didn't place, I would win the world championship. That went back to respecting the barrier and focusing on fundamentals. Then we had to hope that Cash Myers wouldn't place. I told Dad that we needed that steer to win the round, and if I got that steer, I was going for the go-round win and first place overall. The steer that I wanted was a time bomb. He was going to stop right out of the box. It would be like catching a mailbox

A brief family celebration after winning the world championship.

from your pick-up truck doing 45 miles per hour. As soon as I crossed the barrier, I had to be getting off my horse. That might not have been the steer Dad wanted, but it was the steer I needed. I told Dad that if you wanted to win the heavyweight championship of the world, then you had to fight the best. A champion didn't show up for the title fight to make a good showing. A champion showed up to take the title.

The night before the 10$^{th}$ round, we all went to see Shane's show again at the Orleans. I had a few beverages and then went to my room around 11:00. I thought about the next round as I lay there in bed. My thoughts were on that gold buckle. I never rodeoed for the money. That wasn't the main deal to me. I was after the buckle where the silver never tarnished. That was because there was absolutely no silver in it.

**When I woke up Sunday morning, I knew that winning was all I cared about and nothing else would be acceptable. Second place was not an option for me.**

I took my cold shower and shadowboxed my way into an adrenaline-laced frenzy. I got dressed and Jamie pinned my number on my back. I jumped in the limo with Bryan Fields for our daily trip to the Thomas and Mack. Fields had a good Finals, but just hadn't drawn the steers to be in the hunt for a title. (Though I'm sure he someday will.) We talked about wanting steer number 36. Sleepy agreed that number 36 would do the trick. He got this funny little smirk on his face and asked me if I was going to get a case of the big head if I won the title.

I said, "Bro, if they'll let me win this deal, you won't have to worry about seeing me at the rodeos anymore." I was going to take my world title and head home.

You find out who your friends are at critical moments in your life. As soon as I arrived, Jason Lahr, a three-time NFR qualifier, ran up to me and yelled that I drew the steer that Pace and Jones had won their rounds on. "You got him, Sid! You got him, man!" Jason exclaimed again and again. Jason gave me a giant bear hug. He was genuinely excited for me.

"I got what?" I kept asking.

"Number 36! You got the steer, man!"

"You're happy for me?" I asked. I wasn't sure right then if I would have been as happy for someone else as Jason was for me.

I called Dad after the steers had been drawn. My hands were trembling and I told him, "We got 'im!" It was on! Dad didn't say anything. There was a moment of silence. I wanted Dad to know one thing. I wanted that steer, and I

My dad with the family's two championship gold buckles.

wasn't about to blow this deal in the 10th round. Dad was more nervous than I was, and I wanted him to know that I was all right. I was better than all right. Sometimes drawing a good steer is the hard part; throwing this one down would be easy.

**I was after the buckle where the silver never tarnished. That was because there was absolutely no silver in it.**

I called two more people before the 10th round. I called Todd Fox and told him about number 36. He told me to wrap it up. That steer had landed on my table for a reason. Fox knew what he was talking about, and I felt like he was getting another shot. I wanted to win the title for many reasons, and Todd Fox was at the top of the list.

I called Byron Walker before the perf started. Walker told me to stay on the offensive, don't back off. That was great advice. A lot of times when things seem easy, they become the hardest. He said, "Back in there and win the go-round. The average and world title will take care of themselves."

That was it. I was done talking and ready to get on with it. I didn't talk to anyone else before the Grand Entry. I didn't want anyone putting doubts in my mind. I realized that for the first time in my life I had the opportunity to dictate the direction my life would take. Before the 10th round at the NFR, all the bets were off. Your friends were your friends, and the ones who you thought were your friends were nowhere to be found.

Before I got on my horse, one more guy came up to me. Cash Myers flagged me down before the Grand Entry.

"Good luck, Sid." Myers stuck out his hand.

"Thanks, you too," I said. As he started to walk away, I grabbed him and said, "Cash, if I don't win this thing, I hope you do. You are the only one that wouldn't piss me off if you win. If I lose to anyone else, I'll know that I beat myself today."

"I feel the same way, bro!" He turned for his horse and I grabbed mine.

Bill Pace and K. C. Jones were both still in the hunt for the title, but if they beat me, it meant I hadn't done my job. They are both good friends to this day, but Myers was the man that I felt was the one to beat. I am taking nothing away from Pace and Jones. I can only reflect on the way I felt going into the 10th round.

The 10th round was run in order of the world standings. The contestant ranked 15th in the world went first. The order played to the crowd. I was fifth in the world going into the 10th round. That meant I was going to go in the 10th position during the round.

Everyone was nervous. My family had the same seats as they had during the eighth round. Because I had won the eighth round, everyone was happy about the seating arrangements. Nothing is overlooked in rodeo when surveying the karma necessary to win a title.

**That was great advice. A lot of times when things seem easy, they become the hardest.**

But Jamie had a dilemma brewing. Before the first round of the Finals, Jamie had a beer. I did very well in the first round, placed third, and got a nice check. Because no one wanted to break habits when things went well, Jamie had a beer before each round of the Finals. By the 10th round, the string appeared to be working. The problem arose when the 10th round began at 2:00 P.M. on a Sunday afternoon. For Jamie to follow the habits of each round, she would have to drink a beer at 11:30 A.M. Jamie was not a beer drinker and certainly not a morning beer drinker. Although I was not aware of the beer-drinking rituals at the time, I have come to discover that my wife is a bit of a risk-taker. Jamie wanted to soak in every minute of the final round and wanted to remember everything with clear eyes and a keen eye for every detail. Jamie wrestled with the beer decision, then came to the conclusion that if my rodeo future depended on the consumption of one beer, then the world was too screwed up for her to matter much. Jamie declined to have a beer and didn't tell me until after the final round. Dad bit the bullet and swallowed a hot dog.

Watching 10 guys go before me in the 10th round was pure torture. My lungs were burning. I had so much oxygen going through my system that I thought I would explode at any time. I wanted to get on my horse so badly that I could barely control my nerves. Horses sense what we feel. Shady sensed that I was uneasy. I couldn't get him into the corner. The horse was moving all over the box. I had my two friends helping me. I told them earlier that if Shady didn't settle quickly, then they were to jam his butt back into the corner. Herbert Theriot and Mack Altizer were two

**Jamie wrestled with the beer decision, then came to the conclusion that if my rodeo future depended on the consumption of one beer, then the world was too screwed up for her to matter much.**

guys I trusted beyond reproach. Theriot was a former world champion calf-roper and had made the steer wrestling Finals four or five times before. Altizer owned Bad Company Rodeo and was a great friend to my family. I knew that they would have my back at all times. Contestants had corner help for every round, but we had a special meeting before the 10th round. I told Theriot and Altizer that I was nervous, which was an understatement ranked up there with asking Roberto Duran if he liked to mix it up. Shady had a tendency to get jittery at crucial times. My friends knew that.

Everyone was a wreck when it came time for me to go. My family could barely stand to watch. I felt like I was going to explode. I had a hard time positioning Shady in the box. Theriot and Altizer did a great job holding Shady in the corner. When Shady was finally jammed into the corner, I hit my heart with my fist. All the noise stopped. A cool calm came over me, and I settled with the horse. I had never experienced anything like that before. If I could have described the notion of zoned out, that's what I was. I knew that Myers had a good steer. I knew that I had to make a good run to put the heat on him. It was time to go!

The Steiner boys gather 'round the 2002 world-championship saddle.

I barely cleared the barrier and my steer did exactly what I thought he would do. I caught him clean and stuffed him. Every hot summer practice run and every long dreary highway came through my veins. My time was 3.3 seconds, and the arena erupted with an ovation that still rings in my ears to this day. I knew that I had done everything I could have done. I made it back to the box, and

**All the noise stopped. A cool calm came over me, and I settled with the horse. I had never experienced anything like that before.**

everyone was grabbing me and congratulating me. I grabbed Sleepy and asked him if it was over.

Luke Branquinho was up after me. He went into the 10th round first in the world, but out of the average. He told me something before the 10th round that I'll never forget.

"You know what the worst feeling in the world is?" Luke asked me.

"What's that?" I was confused by the question.

"The worst feeling in the world is going into the 10th round in first place without a chance to win the world championship. It's a horrible feeling, but the only thing that makes it a little better is knowing that a good friend has a chance to."

Now that's a good friend. I thought of that conversation when Branquinho rode in the final round. Bill Pace went

The 2002 National Rodeo Finals World Champions. (Photo courtesy of Mike Copeman Photography)

after Branquinho, and Sleepy came up and told me that I was the champ. Cash Myers still had to go. He needed a time of 4.1 seconds to take the title. He ran his steer too far down the arena and didn't place in the 10$^{th}$ round. I was 3.3 for first in the go, and I won the average. The deal was done. I was the 2002 world champion steer wrestler. I was numb. Everyone was slapping me, and I can never remember being physically drained to that extent before.

I took my victory lap and ripped my shirt off. The next thing that I remember was the championship saddles dropping down from the rafters of the Thomas and Mack Center.

The average saddle presentation began immediately after the bull riding. The award presentations for the world champions in each event began later. The contestant who won the average for each event was given a saddle and a buckle for winning the average. Each champion received a saddle and a buckle for their event. What a day! I won the 10th round, I won the average title, and I won the world title.

The media was all around me. I talked to as many people as I could, but I finally told them all that I would return. I had to go see my family for a personal visit. I took off running. I ran so hard to the corridors of the Thomas and Mack. My family was waiting there for me. When they all came into view, I took my hat off and tossed it in the air. We all jumped into each other's arms. We were all crying, and it was simply an indescribable gathering of my family that could never be duplicated. I don't think that Dad cried when he won the world title. He had been riding bulls since he was a little boy, and he expected to be a champion some day. My road was different. I grew up with a champion, and when I began to rodeo, it became more apparent to me that his championship was not only an important part of my life, but an inspiration as well. I never went out to prove anything to the Professional Rodeo Cowboys Association. I went out to prove something to my family and to myself. When I finished an interview, I was described as a good cowboy beyond the long hair and the tattoos. I never understood how the hair and the tattoos made me any less of a cowboy; I didn't try to analyze the media on that day.

I knew at that moment that I did not have it in me to go out on the road again. I may never find that desire again, but I knew that Rocker's and Steely's dad, Jamie's husband, Joleen and Bobby's son, and Shane's brother was a damn good cowboy on a December afternoon in 2002.

# Epilogue

# One-on-One with Sid

The story of 2002 World Champion Steer Wrestler Sid Steiner is the story of an incredible family and one unique young man. I knew that I made a good decision to collaborate on the book after meeting Sid Steiner and his family on my very first visit.

I was granted complete access to the family, and the Steiners are a group that has always preferred quiet resolve to shouting bravado. During our negotiations with one major publisher, a 28-year-old cowboy gave me a lesson in Texas etiquette. When Sid was pressed to bring in another collaborator of their choosing, Sid told a pretentious New York editor to get screwed. I had to step back and reassess the wise one in our relationship. Sid tossed a Texas solution on a Madison Avenue faux pas and signed up a friend for life.

The stars lined up right when Chicago-based Triumph Books decided that Sid Steiner was not a regional icon reserved for the rodeo legions. Triumph knew that Sid

Sid and James Pomerantz.

Steiner was a breath of fresh air amidst a national epidemic of prima donna athletes.

The Steiner family represented a Norman Rockwell portrait, exuding tradition and strength. Family comes first in Bastrop, Texas. Accountability was not a forgotten trend, but a foundation for each child. Children were not financial burdens, but friends for life. For the Steiners, integrity is not a goal. Integrity is a genetic tradition. I asked Sid to sit down and conclude the book with a one-on-one interview.

**Pomerantz:** Why did you want a book written about your life?

**Steiner:** When we talked early in this process, you asked me if I wanted a book to be written about the aspects of my life up until the age of 29. The answer was yes, although I truly believe that the highlights of my life will continue on for years to come. I want everyone to know the fire that burns inside me. I want everyone to know just how cool my family is. I want my kids to pick up this book and show their friends what their family is all about. I want people to know that Sid Rock is not some heathen with cornrowed hair and a quick temper.

**Pomerantz:** Why is Texas such a good place to live? What is it about Texas that is most misunderstood?

**Steiner:** Obviously, the most misunderstood aspect of Texas is that we are all not driving big Cadillacs with horns across the hoods. We are all not shit-kickers with oversized cowboy hats and snakeskin boots. The common visual on Texas is from all the Western movies where they show windswept tumbleweed and prairie dust. That's not Texas. There are places in Texas that look like that, but Texas has some of the prettiest landscapes in our nation. Texas is a state of mind. People are friendlier in Texas. We say yes ma'am, no sir, please, and thank you. I can't tell you how many times when I have ordered in a restaurant that the server turned to me and announced that I must be from Texas because I was polite. I don't see anything wrong with that. I was proud to say, yes I am from Texas. Texas is like our own country. We fly our state flag as high as the American flag. We are a proud state and make no apologies for where we come from. Texas sends more competitors to the NFR each year than any other state. The goose bumps crawled up and down my arms when I rode in the NFR Grand Entry behind the Texas flag.

**Pomerantz:** Do Texans support the president because he is from Texas? That is, do Texans feel an obligation to support the president even if his policies do not agree with the local population?

**Steiner:** I am not here to speak for all Texans. Do I support the president because he is from Texas? Hell, yes! My brother has done things that I couldn't stand, but I fell in right behind him, regardless. George W. Bush is a brother. We all go to battle for each other. Does that mean that I agree with everything he has done? No, but we stick together in Texas. Don't forget that.

**Pomerantz:** Talk about the current state of the Professional Rodeo Cowboys Association (PRCA). You won the 2002 world championship and then retired from competition. Why?

**Steiner:** First of all, I accomplished everything that I set out to do in rodeo. I never told anyone that I wanted to win two, three, or eight straight world titles. I wanted to win one. When Ty Murray grew up, his sights were set on winning more all-around championships than anyone else in the world. Well, Ty set his sights pretty high. Larry Mahan had won six. I had my sights set on one. After I had won one, there was not the fire beneath me that is so necessary to continue to make the sacrifices that each of us has to make to have a chance to secure a world title.

My dad had gone out on top. I always thought that was very cool. Dad told me that if he had the same opportunities available today, that he may not have retired right away. I thought about all those opportunities. I had many sponsor deals pending when I quit. Then I looked at my little girl and thought about dragging her all over the country month after month. How fair was it to take Steely away from her grandparents? Jamie's mom moved to Bastrop recently. Steely has everyone here. If given a choice, I am certain that she wouldn't want to leave.

So, do I tell my family, "I have achieved everything I dreamed about in rodeo, but I'm still going to be on the road even if it doesn't make sense financially. Life on the road isn't that bad." Christ, it is that bad for me! It is not a place to raise my kids. I am not passing judgment on other competitors. I have great friends that have chosen rodeo for their lives and I respect their decisions. They are great dads and moms, but that is not my choice. I loved winning a world title, but it is time to raise my kids to be world champions in whatever they choose to do. I want them to know their father. I don't want their memories of me to be only the holidays and the sporadic breaks in the grueling rodeo schedule.

**Pomerantz:** Do you think there will be a competitive void that you will find hard to fill without rodeo?

**Steiner:** Hell, yes! That's why when that light turns green, I jump on the pedal and try to crush that sucker next to me. Just kidding. I still lift weights and water-ski like hell every chance I get. Rodeo is not the only way to compete. It was harder after the Finals and the new season started. My friends called me from every rodeo, and they were there and I was here. I missed winning, and I missed the adrenaline of waiting to run that Saturday night perf.

**Pomerantz:** The PRCA has changed dramatically the number of rodeos that can count toward the season money total. How have the new rules affected the sport? How did the new rules affect your decision to quit?

**Steiner:** Look, the PRCA does not need Sid Steiner to give them any advice. Our sport has grown tremendously over the past decade. With that in mind, I do have an opinion. The new rules suck. I am so glad that I won the title in 2002, the last year before they changed the rules. When I competed, I wanted to get it on all the time. If we were going to rodeo, then let's find out who was the best at every venue. We tried to get to 100 rodeos. Now, you can only count 50 rodeos to the final rankings. The money is better for the bigger events, but theoretically a cowboy could make the Finals with as little as 20 rodeos. That doesn't seem right to me. The Finals should be an attrition test to find out who is the best everywhere.

**Pomerantz:** Why did they invoke the new rules?

**Steiner:** The objective was to ease the travel burden on the competitors and make sure that more of the bigger names got to the bigger money rodeos.

**Pomerantz:** That seems logical. Did they succeed?

**Steiner:** No. Let's say that I was traveling to a rodeo in Kennewick, Washington, with my truck, my hazer, my trailer, and my horses. The rodeo was on the first weekend of the month. The next rodeo I could enter was held two weeks later in Caldwell, Idaho. Do you think I would drive back to Austin, stay for a couple days, and then drive back to Idaho for another weekend rodeo? When there were no limits, we would make use of all the time on the road. I would have entered three or four smaller rodeos in between the bigger events. At least we were making money and not sitting around. Now, we would have to stay out on the road incurring more expenses because the travel back and forth from the northwest to Texas would be too much. The smaller rodeos are now deprived of the bigger names because we are limited to 50 rodeos. It is a lose-lose situation. The premise for the new rules was sound, but the new rules don't consider distance and downtime.

The biggest hurdle within rodeo today, in my opinion, is that there is not one solution for the sport. There are too many people making good money now, and the PRCA administration cannot make one or two changes to please everyone. Look, I am not an expert on what the sport of rodeo needs or doesn't need. I am not here to bad-mouth the sport that fulfilled my dreams and provided so many outstanding relationships and memories. Every sport has some issues.

**Pomerantz:** Is it too expensive for many to compete at a high level in rodeo? In other words, is the formula upside down for many competitors?

**Steiner:** There is the money issue. We are not making enough money, period. Entry fees are up. Fuel costs are up. Prices for good horses are way up. Vehicle costs are up. The prize money in most rodeos has changed very little in 20 years. We are making the same money, and we are spending much more to earn it. I did not pursue rodeo to become a rich man. I wanted to accomplish a goal. After I had accomplished that goal, I had to think about where I was going to make the most money. Rodeo was not the first choice. If I were single, maybe things would be different, but I'm not single. In high school, I was voted the most likely to mooch off my parents. Surprisingly, I had more ambitious plans. I did appreciate the award, but it did not come as a shock. Mom asked me why the award was not a shock. I said because Shane won it the year before. I was a shoo-in.

**Pomerantz:** What effect did the Professional Bull Riders (PBR) have on the PRCA?

**Steiner:** None.

**Pomerantz:** Haven't they achieved a financial level that exceeds the PRCA?

**Steiner:** Bullriding has always been the most dangerous event and the most popular. We are a nation that loves wrecks. That's why we love NASCAR. Do you think that people are into the splendid colors of the cars or the nonstop action of watching cars chase each other around a track? They are waiting for the wrecks. What better premise for that than a man against a 2,000-pound animal. People have died bullriding. The PBR has done a good job in getting their riders in front of their fans. The same guys compete at each event. The public begins to get to know personalities. Sports are personality-driven. PBR fans begin to root for Chris Shivers or Adriano Moreas or Ross Coleman. Television coverage is everything to bringing the sport to the public. The PRCA has fewer prime-time hours than the PBR, more events, and a more difficult task to get the public to know the competitors.

**Pomerantz:** Wasn't that where you came in? Finally, rodeo had a marketable personality?

**Steiner:** Maybe I gave the sport some more visibility, but the same problems were there.

**Pomerantz:** By cutting the number of rodeos, wouldn't that increase the likelihood of the best competitors meeting at fewer rodeos? Wouldn't that scenario create the ability to promote more personalities? The same guys would be together more.

**Steiner:** Theoretically, yes. In reality, in the scramble for the fewer number of big-money rodeos, the entry numbers grew. If we keep sending more guys to the same rodeos, then most of the competitors performed in the slack rounds and were never in front of the cameras or the bigger audiences of Friday and Saturday night. The slack rounds used to be held to accommodate the rodeo jockeying, for squeezing as many rodeos as possible into each weekend. Now it seems that the slack rounds may only be for the overflow of entries.

**Pomerantz:** Do you think that there is a perception across the country that rodeo is a cruel sport?

**Steiner:** Obviously there is some of that. The animal rights groups have not helped the sport because they don't know the sport. The best way to understand how the animals are treated is to look at the stock contractors. These people make their money when they provide quality animals that perform at their best. The stock contractors treat the horses and bulls like star athletes because they are. The stories about mistreating rodeo livestock are mostly fiction. Have there ever been bad operators in rodeo that mistreated the livestock? Sure, but they are long gone in PRCA competition. No one ties ropes around the bulls' testicles to make them buck. The rope is called a "flank rope," and it is tied across the animal's stomach, about six inches in front of the animal's testicles. The rope does nothing but tickle the animal. The sensation makes for a better bucking bronc or bull.

**Pomerantz:** Is rodeo an American institution?

**Steiner:** I think rodeo is a great myth. No one wants it to go away. Most people don't understand the sport and that adds to the appeal. Who hasn't been a cowboy when they were a kid?

**Pomerantz:** Would you object to your children chasing their rodeo dreams? With a father and a grandfather as world champions, the temptation may arise.

**Steiner:** My kids can do whatever they want to do. I have done rodeo. I want my kids to do something better than me.

**Pomerantz:** Would you steer your kids away from rodeo?

**Steiner:** I would steer them away, but they will follow their own hearts. It is dangerous, and it takes them away from Jamie and me. Why would I encourage them to leave?

**Pomerantz:** Which rodeo competitors have you admired the most, besides your father?

**Steiner:** Ty Murray comes to mind first. Ty took things to another level. To excel at that many events and stay healthy as long as he did was, without question, a standard that our sport may never see again. I admired George Paul. I never met George Paul, but Dad told me stories about the kind of man he was. I admire Larry Mahan. He was the first guy to show everyone that you could be a good cowboy and dress a little different and have long hair. I can never answer this question without mentioning Todd Fox.

**Pomerantz:** Do you enjoy watching rodeo?

**Steiner:** I enjoy watching my friends compete.

**216**

**Pomerantz:** Sid, we have danced around with the subject a bit, but let's get to it. Are you finished competing as a bulldogger on the PRCA Tour?

**Steiner:** Yes, if we are talking about the current rules and conditions. I am not prepared to go out and compete under the same rules and prize money that exist today. If things in rodeo drastically changed, then I would certainly look at the changes and evaluate how those circumstances related to my family and me. Don't look for the PRCA to change anything in rodeo to please Sid Steiner. I would not expect them to. I have not been competing long enough to be an expert on the changes that would help rodeo the most. I know what changes have affected me, that's all.

**Pomerantz:** There are many people following rodeo who are going to miss you on tour. In the eight years that you competed, I cannot remember anyone creating such a groundswell of support and outrage that shadowed your career. Most of those fans do not want to see your career over just when it got rolling. Can they do anything to change your mind about retiring?

**Steiner:** I am not on a campaign to change rodeo, and while I love the support, there are a whole lot of issues more important than whether I compete again. The entire system works for many, many people. The one constant that I would like to see change is the way cowboys are paid. Rodeo is the only sport where the competitors put up the money. Rodeo entry fees make up the prize money at most rodeos. Sponsorship money comes into play at the bigger venues, but the old system is still alive and well for most of the rodeo tour. You will not see the PGA golfers throwing their own money into The Masters pot.

**Pomerantz:** Is rodeo too accessible for anyone to compete? I mean, if I got a PRCA permit, then I could compete at the same rodeos that you were entered. Anyone can get a PRCA permit, right?

**Steiner:** Any college rodeo athlete or noncollege rodeo athlete can become a professional rodeo competitor if they buy a PRCA permit. They can become a full-time professional rodeo competitor if they win a minimum of $1,000 in a year to fill their permits. Hell, I did it with little or no experience. I dedicated myself to winning, and I was prepared to do anything it took to become the best, but most young rodeo hopefuls just want the experience. Imagine getting a golf PGA permit for $1,000 and entering the Players Championship tournament in Florida. You and Tiger would be in the same tournament. It happens in rodeo.

**Pomerantz:** What is the best format in rodeo?

**Steiner:** Outside of the NFR, it's Houston without a doubt.

**Pomerantz:** Why is Houston different?

**Steiner:** Houston takes the top 50 competitors from each event. The list is based on the past year's rankings.

Each year, some fall off the list and some new ones join it. The system is not unlike the PGA Tour with the Buy.Com Tour, or NASCAR and the Busch Grand National Tour. Rodeo could take a page from those sports and develop more than one level of competition. It would be easier to market stars, and the public would grow to know some of the competitors.

**Pomerantz:** Is it fun to be a world champion?

**Steiner:** Absolutely, but I retired right after I won, so I didn't get a chance to travel with the guys as a world champion. I think about that some days. Like I said, it's fun to daydream. I do want to thank everyone that played a part in the most exciting eight-year run of my life. I will miss the fans, most of whom supported me through the good and the bad runs. They made this trip fun. You all know by now that my family is very important to me and I have found a bigger family across the country than I ever imagined possible. The PRCA has supported me when it counted most, and I thank them for believing in the fans first. I want to thank all the cowboys competing at rodeos across the country. I will miss the competitors more than I can describe. The world title is an exciting memory and a tremendous personal achievement, but the relationships forged on the road and at the arenas across the country are the trophies that I will cherish the most. If I see you down the road, we'll have some more fun. If not, thanks for the ride.

# Appendix

## Standings for the 2002 Wrangler National Finals in Steer Wrestling

**First Round:** 1. Luke Branquinho, 3.9 seconds, $13,923; 2. Jason Lahr, 4.0, $11,003; 3. Sid Steiner, 4.1, $8,309; 4. Birch Neggard, 4.2, $5,839; 5. (tie) Cash Myers and Lee Graves, 4.4, $2,919 each; 7. Bryan Fields, 4.7; 8. (tie) Bill Pace, K. C. Jones, and Rod Lyman, 5.0; 11. Todd Suhn, 5.2; 12. Ivon Nelson, 6.4; 13. (tie) Joey Bell Jr., Curtis Cassidy, and Bob Lummus, no time.

**Second Round:** 1. Birch Neggard, 3.6 seconds, $13,923; 2. Rod Lyman, 3.8, $11,003; 3. Cash Myers, 3.9, $8,309; 4. Joey Bell Jr., 4.1, $5,839; 5. Sid Steiner, 4.4, $3,593; 6. K. C. Jones, 4.6, $2,246; 7. (tie) Bill Pace, Luke Branquinho, and Ivon

Nelson, 4.7; 10. Bob Lummus, 5.0; 11. Lee Graves, 5.1; 12. Bryan Fields, 5.3; 13. Todd Suhn, 5.5; 14. (tie) Curtis Cassidy and Jason Lahr, no time.

**Third Round:** 1. Joey Bell Jr., 3.6 seconds, $13,923; 2. Bill Pace, 3.8, $11,003; 3. K. C. Jones, 3.9, $8,309; 4. (tie) Sid Steiner and Todd Suhn, 4.0, $4,716 each; 6. Cash Myers, 4.1, $2,246; 7. Lee Graves, 4.4; 8. (tie) Rod Lyman and Birch Neggard, 4.5; 10. (tie) Luke Branquinho and Ivon Nelson, 4.6; 12. Bob Lummus, 6.6; 13. (tie) Curtis Cassidy, Bryan Fields, and Jason Lahr, no time.

**Fourth Round:** 1. K. C. Jones, 3.7 seconds, $13,923; 2. Birch Neggard, 3.9, $11,003; 3. (tie) Cash Myers and Lee Graves, 4.0, $7,074 each; 5. (tie) Bill Pace and Sid Steiner, 4.2, $2,919 each; 7. Bob Lummus, 4.3; 8. (tie) Bryan Fields and Ivon Nelson, 4.5; 10. Jason Lahr, 4.6; 11. Joey Bell Jr., 4.7; 12. Todd Suhn, 4.8; 13. Curtis Cassidy, 5.9; 14. (tie) Rod Lyman and Luke Branquinho, no time.

**Fifth Round:** 1. Rod Lyman, 3.8 seconds, $13,923; 2. (tie) Luke Branquinho and Bryan Fields, 3.9, $9,656 each; 4. Todd Suhn, 4.2, $5,839; 5. Sid Steiner, 4.3, $3,593; 6. Birch Neggard, 4.4, $2,246; 7. Jason Lahr , 4.5; 8. Lee Graves, 4.7; 9. Bill Pace, 4.8; 10. K. C. Jones, 4.9; 11. Cash Myers, 5.0; 12. Joey Bell Jr., 14.0; 13. Ivon Nelson, 15.5; 14. (tie) Curtis Cassidy and Bob Lummus, no time.

**Sixth Round:** 1. Rod Lyman, 3.3 seconds, $13,923; 2. Birch Neggard, 3.4, $11,003; 3. Curtis Cassidy, 3.6, $8,309; 4. (tie) Joey Bell Jr. and Lee Graves, 3.7, $4,716 each; 6. Cash Myers, 3.8, $2,246; 7. (tie) Bob Lummus and K. C. Jones, 3.9; 9. (tie) Bill Pace and Ivon Nelson, 4.3; 11. Jason Lahr, 4.5; 12. Sid Steiner, 4.9; 13. Todd Suhn, 5.5; 14. Luke Branquinho, 5.9; 15. Bryan Fields, 6.2.

**Seventh Round:** 1. Bill Pace, 3.5 seconds, $13,923; 2. Todd Suhn, 3.9, $11,003; 3. (tie) Bob Lummus and Luke Branquinho, 4.0, $7,074 each; 5. Curtis Cassidy, 4.2, $3,593; 6. Jason Lahr, 4.3, $2,246; 7. Cash Myers, 4.4; 8. Ivon Nelson, 4.5; 9. K. C. Jones, 4.7; 10. Sid Steiner, 5.0; 11. (tie) Rod Lyman, Lee Graves, and Birch Neggard, 5.5; 14. Joey Bell Jr., 14.2; 15. Bryan Fields, no time.

**Eighth Round:** 1. Sid Steiner, 3.6 seconds, $13,923; 2. (tie) Luke Branquinho and Jason Lahr, 3.7, $9,656 each; 4. Joey Bell Jr., 3.9, $5,839; 5. Bryan Fields, 4.1, $3,593; 6. Bill Pace, 4.2, $2,246; 7. Todd Suhn, 4.3; 8. (tie) Cash Myers and Ivon Nelson, 4.4; 10. Bob Lummus, 4.5; 11. K. C. Jones, 4.6; 12. Lee Graves, 4.9; 13. Curtis Cassidy, 5.2; 14. (tie) Rod Lyman and Birch Neggard, no time.

**Ninth Round:** 1. Luke Branquinho, 3.5 seconds, $13,923; 2. Ivon Nelson, 3.6, $11,003; 3. (tie) Cash Myers, K. C. Jones, and Bryan Fields, 3.7, $5,913 each; 6. (tie) Sid Steiner and Birch Neggard, 4.0, $1,123 each; 8. Joey Bell Jr., 4.2; 9. Curtis Cassidy, 4.3; 10. (tie) Rod Lyman and Jason Lahr, 4.4; 12. Bill Pace, 5.0; 13. Todd Suhn, 5.2; 14. Bob Lummus, 6.2; 15. Lee Graves, 13.3.

**Tenth Round:** 1. Sid Steiner, 3.3 seconds, $13,923; 2. Ivon Nelson, 3.6, $11,003; 3. Bryan Fields, 3.8, $8,309; 4. Lee Graves, 3.9, $5,839; 5. Birch Neggard, 4.1, $3,593; 6. Curtis Cassidy, 4.3, $2,246; 7. Bill Pace, 4.6; 8. Bob Lummus, 4.8; 9. Luke Branquinho, 5.0; 10. Cash Myers, 5.1; 11. Todd Suhn, 7.3; 12. Rod Lyman, 13.7; 13. Jason Lahr, 13.8; 14. K. C. Jones, 14.3; 15. Joey Bell Jr., no time.

**World champion:** Sid Steiner, $162,516.

**Average champion:** Sid Steiner, 41.80 seconds on 10 head.

# Index

*Numbers in italics refer to photographs.*